A Manifesto for Ombudsman Reform

"Since the first ombudsman reached our shores in 1967, ombudsmen have proliferated and proved popular and successful. From time to time, ombudsmen have popped up in private and public contexts—we cannot talk of a public ombudsman system. A draft Public Ombudsmen Bill which was on the table was crowded out by Brexit.

Back to the drawing board. The editors and authors of the present book advocate deeper and more systematic change. All have studied ombudsmen over many years and all who read this scholarly book will agree that no one is better qualified. Roll on reform, please!"

—Carol Harlow, *London School of Economics, London, UK*

Richard Kirkham • Chris Gill
Editors

A Manifesto for Ombudsman Reform

palgrave
macmillan

Editors
Richard Kirkham
Sheffield University
Sheffield, UK

Chris Gill
University of Glasgow
Glasgow, UK

ISBN 978-3-030-40611-0 ISBN 978-3-030-40612-7 (eBook)
https://doi.org/10.1007/978-3-030-40612-7

Cover illustration: Ben Miners/Getty

This Palgrave Pivot imprint is published by the registered company Springer Nature Switzerland AG.
The registered company address is: Gewerbestrasse 11, 6330 Cham, Switzerland

Foreword

This publication is not only timely—it may represent a final chance to bring the Ombudsman system in England into the twenty-first century. Not all the answers are here but the main questions are, and are posed well.

The debate over whether the people of England should benefit from a Public Services Ombudsman has been running now for two decades or more. These discussions have been closed and narrow focusing on the shortcomings of individual Ombudsman schemes plying their trade in England. Rarely have they focused on the public's needs or potential benefits of reform to the people of England or its public bodies.

Politicians, academics, and it must also be said practitioners, particularly at the Parliamentary and Health Service Ombudsman (PHSO) until the relatively recent arrival of Rob Behrens as Ombudsman, have whiled away the 2000s tinkering with the old, broken system while any serious consideration of a new Ombudsman model and new ways of working were rarely considered. Even in times of crisis, the two principal public Ombudsman schemes in England, the Local Government Ombudsman (LGO) and the PHSO, have had their share of crises in the last ten years; the main focus has been on addressing short-term problems with internal and functional rather than strategic solutions.

Grey sky thinking has bedevilled the debate.

Until the publication of this compendium, the academic community has in my view tended to let the sector and the people who depend on it down. They created for themselves a safe space where researchers became comfortable replicating internal audit functions and offering management advice, rather than tackling the big, forward looking issues. They lost sight of their real role.

Indeed, as constitutional change swept the UK as a result of devolution, bringing with it different structures and methods, and a redefinition of the role of Public Service Ombudsman schemes in Northern Ireland, Wales, and Scotland, many in the academic community took the view that these developments were an aberration and not what 'real Ombudsman schemes' do.

The gold standard was of course the PHSO model. Practically unchanged in its culture since the 1960s, the PHSO was seen as the lead UK body sitting atop a pyramid of schemes, to whose methods and values all other schemes should aspire.

Entering this world, leading a relatively new scheme in the UK, and advocating for a more focused, user friendly approach, one which can enable public bodies to learn and improve by engaging with them in the public interest, and advocating for similar change elsewhere often felt like swearing in church.

But there is no getting away from it. The institution that was the PHSO, and the system it was such a leading part of, had lost touch with the positive changes that were happening elsewhere in the UK and in the rest of the Ombudsman world. It had forgotten how to develop and had been left behind. Not just by nouveau upstart schemes in the rest of the UK, but by exciting developing schemes across the world in places like Australia, Canada, and in Europe.

As other schemes were pushing forward, Ombudsman schemes in England were losing the confidence of the people and organisations they were there to serve. They were met by accusations of poor performance, low public esteem, headline making failures, and a general dissatisfaction with the service they provided.

It was seen to be a failing sector. It almost certainly was.

To those of us looking in from outside, this was not just about a catalogue of individual failures, but a clear sign of systemic failure. Yet the dots have still remained un-joined for far too long by Ombudsman scheme leaders, politicians, and academics whose roles should have enabled them to analyse the problem strategically. They were, and many still are, still trying to fix Ombudsman institutions rather than fixing the service.

In the face of severe public and parliamentary criticism the LGO was pressed by a select committee to completely revise its governance and operational methods amid draconian budget cuts. The impact on LGO and its culture was devastating, though it has emerged as a stronger organisation more receptive to change.

As for the PHSO, its position as the leading Ombudsman institution in the UK became no longer credible as cracks began to appear in its processes, while simultaneously its public image rapidly declined. Its stiff adherence to a definition of what an Ombudsman is, framed in the cautious language of 1960s Parliamentary speak, was out of step with modern world. Yet insiders, and many academics, not only failed to recognise that the world had moved on, but determined instead to circle their wagons and argue for the one true model.

Many of us outside England were left shaking our heads in despair.

The PHSO and the style of Ombudsman scheme it represented had fallen, in a relatively short period of time, from a valued part of the system of public scrutiny of government, to a body, seemingly left behind by events, trying hard to find its purpose in a world it was never designed to serve. Where changes in the dynamics, structure, and delivery of government across the UK, and the pace and the complexities of our modern health service have challenged almost fatally its slow paced, one-size-fits-all model.

That the PHSO model held its pre-eminent position for so long is remarkable given its inherent resistance to change. That is almost certainly down to its close relationship with the UK Parliament, to the strong personal position of the Ombudsman in the early period of this century, Ann Abraham, and to a number of one off investigations she led, including the investigation into the Equitable Life pensions debacle.

But these set play successes masked a deeper problem. In the period after her departure, the public profile Ann Abraham created was not matched and public confidence in the institution eroded. Indeed, over much of the last decade, the period post Abraham and pre Behrens, many of us feared that its poor performance and the resistance to fundamental change of the PHSO leadership could have put the credibility of the Ombudsman brand itself in danger. Only now is the PHSO beginning its recovery.

But that is not enough. Confusing the future of the PHSO with the future of the Ombudsman service in England is the mistake that has held England back.

The legislative logjam that has followed the Brexit referendum, by thwarting the delivery of timid reform legislation, has given a second opportunity to develop a fresh approach.

The academics who have contributed to this compendium have seized this opportunity to put forward ideas, fresh ideas, about how the system in England might be reformed and improved.

It is a pleasure to see that in the Principles developed here the citizen is at the heart of the thinking and not the management of institutions.

The experience of other jurisdictions who offer a single stop point of entry for citizens to an Ombudsman scheme responsible for all public services, a Public Service Ombudsman, is weighed, evaluated, and proposals made for how experience gained elsewhere might be adapted to meet the English environment. Governance models are considered which are controversial, and clear proposals for change made.

The impact of devolution on the governance of the UK and how Ombudsman schemes should respond to these settled changes is considered carefully and radical thinking in this publication poses questions, not just for the Ombudsman schemes in England but across the nations of the UK.

This is an exciting publication, which offers food for thought on all sides. Not everyone will agree with every conclusion contained here. I for one do not. But this kind of thinking and open debate might have saved the Ombudsman service in England years of angst had it been produced earlier. The compilers and contributors are to be congratulated for their refreshing approach.

There is not a lot of grey sky thinking to be found here.

Lenzie Jim Martin
CBE is Chair of the Scottish Legal Complaints
Commission and a former Scottish
Public Services Ombudsman and Police
Complaints Commissioner for Scotland.
December 2019

Contents

List of Contributors

Naomi Creutzfeldt University of Westminster, London, UK
Chris Gill University of Glasgow, Glasgow, UK
Carolyn Hirst Queen Margaret University, Musselburgh, UK
Richard Kirkham Sheffield University, Sheffield, UK
Nick O'Brien University of Liverpool, Liverpool, UK
Brian Thompson University of Liverpool, Liverpool, UK

Abbreviations

ADR	Alternative Dispute Resolution
C&AG	Comptroller and Auditor General
CSA	Complaint Standards Authority
FOS	Financial Ombudsman Service
HSC	Health Service Commissioner
LGO	Local Government Ombudsman
LGSCO	Local Government and Social Care Ombudsman
MOP	Modern Ombudsman Practice
NAO	National Audit Office
NPM	New Public Management
OIA	Office of the Independent Adjudicator for Higher Education
PAC	Public Accounts Committee
PACAC	Public Administration and Constitutional Affairs Committee
PASC	Public Administration Select Committee
PCA	Parliamentary Commissioner for Administration
PHSO	Parliamentary and Health Service Ombudsman
PSO	Public Services Ombudsman
SPSO	Scottish Public Services Ombudsman
VFM	Value for Money

List of Tables

CHAPTER 1

Introduction

Chris Gill and Richard Kirkham

Abstract This book makes an argument for legislative reform to a number of the public service ombudsman offices operating in the UK, with a particular focus on England. In doing so, it outlines a manifesto for designing the new office that will appeal to policymakers, legislators, ombudsman practitioners, and academics interested in the field of administrative justice. This book provides detailed analysis of some of the main issues that will need to be considered in creating a new public service ombudsman, in part by applying evidence from around the globe. It argues that the current period offers a once in a generation opportunity to reshape the public service ombudsman sector in the UK around a coherent vision of administrative justice, one that enables the office to identify systemic maladministration and promote a more strategic oversight of public administration than is currently possible.

C. Gill (✉)
University of Glasgow, Glasgow, UK
e-mail: Chris.Gill@glasgow.ac.uk

R. Kirkham
Sheffield University, Sheffield, UK
e-mail: r.m.kirkham@sheffield.ac.uk

R. Kirkham, C. Gill (eds.), *A Manifesto for Ombudsman Reform*,
https://doi.org/10.1007/978-3-030-40612-7_1

Keywords Legislative reform • Public Services Ombudsman • Administrative justice • Powers • Institutional design

This book seeks to persuade policymakers and legislators of the need for legislative reform to a number of the public service ombudsman (PSO) offices operating in the UK and to evidence the ways in which that reforming legislation should be designed. In pursuing this goal, this book represents a response to a challenge laid down by the Parliamentary and Health Service Ombudsman, Rob Behrens, at a *JUSTICE* event in February 2018. It was too easy, he said, to blame the legislative logjam caused by Brexit for the failure of the government to implement its 2016 proposal for a new integrated PSO office. The failure had also been caused by the lack of hard evidence to support the need for reform.

In response to this challenge, this book lays out a manifesto for the future that we hope will influence the legislative debate around ombudsman reform and inform academic and policy debates about the future of the institution in the UK. Although containing a clear policy goal, all the chapters of the book are derived and based upon leading research on the ombudsman sector both in the UK and elsewhere. As such, it will appeal to policymakers, practitioners, and academics.

The book offers a guide to the main issues that will need to be considered in developing legislative reforms of the ombudsman sector in the UK. Most of the chapters in the book were first presented at a roundtable event on ombudsman legislative reform held in Sheffield in January 2019, attended by six of the then PSO office-holders in the UK, and a cross-section of academics and stakeholders to the sector. We are extremely thankful to the Nuffield Foundation for funding the event under a research grant held by Richard Kirkham (2017).

In this introductory chapter, we set the scene for the current debates on proposals for a new integrated PSO office and outline the chapters in the book.

Arguments for Legislative Reform

Since first appearing in Britain with the establishment of the Parliamentary Commissioner for Administration (Parliamentary Commissioner Act 1967), PSOs have become an important component in the country's grievance handling machinery. Their introduction formed part of a wider post-war shift towards offering citizens greater protection in their dealings with the state and a means of challenging failures in public service delivery. The perceived need for this shift recognised the value of administrative justice to individual citizens and the collective demos and sought to address declining levels of trust in public administration (Whyatt 1961; Gregory and Giddings 2002: 33–124).

The development of the PSO model within the justice system represented an implicit acceptance that neither the court nor the tribunal system was alone capable of bearing the burden of delivering administrative justice. However, since its establishment, it has become clear that the significance of the PSO role goes wider than individual grievance handling: periodically acting as a powerful voice for citizen and service user concerns, forcing the government to give enhanced credence to demands for good administration and in multiple instances bringing about the redress of systemic maladministration (see Gregory and Giddings 2002).

The strength of these claims to need and impact is such that the PSO has become an integral part of the UK's constitutional order (Abraham 2008). Nevertheless, the time has come for an upgrade to its legislative design to equip it to meet the challenges of twenty-first century governance. The original model for the PSO implemented in the 1967 Act was a limited measure, which carefully calibrated a novel foreign transplant onto the UK's existing Parliamentary and common law constitution. However, it has long been recognised that the model needs upgrading (Kirkham 2007) and for England at least any formal statutory adaptation so far attempted has been minimal. As Jim Martin makes clear in his challenging foreword to this book, the need for reform in England is urgent and requires bold new ideas to be considered. With the administrative justice system in a state of flux and facing fresh challenges, including technological changes, austerity, and rapidly evolving citizen expectations, now is an opportune time for reform and this collection provides a detailed outline of the issues that will need to be addressed in completing this project.

There are four basic drivers for PSO reform (Kirkham and Martin 2014). First, there is a 'tidying-up' rationale. PSO legislation has become outdated in ways that either prevent the development and modernisation of the sector or force it to pursue 'work-around' solutions that can be costly and dysfunctional. Second, since 1967, multiple sector-specific individual PSO offices have been created but the resultant network does not always match the manner in which public services are delivered today (Gordon 2013:

paras. 25–38). This mismatch means that individual PSO offices sometimes struggle to resolve complaints by themselves, leading to complicated joint investigations with other offices. Simultaneously, individual complainants are confronted by a barely comprehensible choice of options by which to pursue their grievance (Public Administration Select Committe (PASC) 2007–2008). Third, there is a broader concern that the wider administrative justice system needs to be better equipped to promote better decision-making within the government, as well as providing individual remedies. PSOs can only ever be a part of the answer here, but a lack of necessary powers places limitations on the institution's current ability to act as a catalyst for improvements in public administration. Fourth, it is argued by some that the current ombudsman system is not delivering for either individual service users or the public service providers under the jurisdiction of PSO (e.g. Doyle and O'Brien 2019; Reynolds 2017). As a result, the PSO design needs to be radically reshaped to secure better outcomes, with a number of alternative solutions proposed.

Notwithstanding the acceptance by key stakeholders of the need for change (e.g. see Cabinet Office 2000; Law Commission 2011; PASC 2013–2014; Gordon 2014: 12–14), the dominant response of the government and Parliament has been to tinker incrementally with the design of the institution by tagging-on extra provisions to existing offices rather than pursue the wide-ranging reforms that are required to achieve real change (e.g. Local Government and Public Involvement Act 2007: ss.168–182; Health Act 2009: s.35, sch.5). Likewise, calls for the expansion in the coverage of the PSO have generally been responded to by introducing new bespoke offices (e.g. in local government, health, prisons, and education) rather than establishing a more powerful integrated office, resulting in eight separate PSOs in England alone (see Chap. 4). In terms of full-scale reform, a 2000 Cabinet Office report proposed a merged 'Parliamentary' PSO for the UK (Cabinet Office 2000: 5–6), but this move ultimately resulted only in a minor measure being applied (Regulatory Reform (Collaboration etc. Between Ombudsmen) Order 2007) which facilitates joint investigations between different offices but adds little else to the office's powers.

Thus, for at least two decades now, there has been widespread agreement that the ombudsman sector in England is in need of a significant shake-up, but there has also been an accompanying unwillingness on the part of government to prioritise that reform in a full scale legislative package. There may have been good reasons for this preference for incremental adjustment over radical reform, as change always carries the potential for unforeseen consequences. The limitations imposed upon the sector by its aged legislation and ad hoc historical development have now reached the stage, however, where they are acting as a barrier to further evolution of best practice.

One riddle that has made the reform more complicated is the asymmetric nature of devolution in the UK. The first UK PSO, the Parliamentary Commissioner for Administration (PCA), has a jurisdiction that covers all nations of the country, and it is important that this is addressed in the process of legislative reform (see Chaps. 2 and 3 on this point). In Northern Ireland, Scotland, and Wales, devolution has led to three separate PSO offices been created, and in turn, this has provided opportunities for significant reform, with the introduction of pioneering initiatives such as 'Complaint Standards Authority' powers and powers of own-initiative investigation. By contrast, in the words of Jim Martin, the former Scottish Public Services Ombudsman, the ombudsman in England was 'stuck in time' (PASC 2013–2014: para. 44). As a result the focus of this book is on England (alongside the UK-wide jurisdiction of the PCA) and we refer to other jurisdictions only insofar as they provide possible models for change and renewal here.

The most recent attempt at reform in England was the draft Public Services Ombudsman Bill ('the draft Bill': Cabinet Office 2016). The draft Bill proposed some sensible measures, allowing for the integration of three offices (plus potentially a fourth) into a new single PSO scheme. But the Bill was widely criticised for being too timid (e.g. Kirkham and Thompson 2017; O'Brien 2019; McBurnie 2017; Reynolds 2017), particularly when compared to legislation in the devolved nations. Since its publication, the draft Bill has become stuck in the legislative logjam that Brexit has created and has probably now joined the list of failed efforts at securing change.

This hiatus has though created a welcome opportunity to develop more extensive and bolder proposals for legislative reform.

What's in a Name?

Before detailing the contents of the book one preliminary point needs to be addressed, which is the increasing smorgasbord of titles that are used to describe PSO in the UK and elsewhere. This is an important issue for reasons of presentational consistency and long-term branding. To cite two leading writers on the topic:

> [O]ne aim of establishing a brand is to promote awareness and understanding among potential consumers to enable them to make a discerning choice. In the context of ombuds, the 'brand' being promoted is associated with reliability, expertise, authority and a number of other features presumed to be desirable. (Bondy and Doyle 2018: 485)

Until recently, the standard assumption in the sector was that promoting a strong 'brand' meant uniformly applying the label 'ombudsman' to all independent complaint-handling schemes that met certain robust criteria (e.g. see Ombudsman Association 2019; McMillan 2008). In New Zealand this is a statutory requirement (Ombudsman Act 1975: s.28A). Likewise, in the UK, in order to protect the brand the rules of Companies House were amended. It is now a requirement that private sector alternative dispute resolution schemes attempting to register as a company with a title including the word 'ombudsman' must be a full member of the Ombudsman Association,[1] the leading association for complaint-handling schemes in the UK and Ireland.

There are, however, two underlying issues with the title 'ombudsman'.

First, there is a debate about the supposed gender specific connotations of the title, with many preferring to use the gender-neutral term ombud(s) or ombudspersons (see Northern Ireland Assembly 2015; Jersey Law Commission 2018: ch.3). Differences of opinion on this issue can be seen in ombudsman literature and, as far as we are aware, amongst practitioners. In this chapter, and the following, for consistency the term ombudsman is used as the dominant reference is to improving upon the 2016 Public Services 'Ombudsman' Bill. In other chapters in the book, however, authors have preferred to use 'ombud(s)' unless referring specifically to a named institution that carries the title 'ombudsman'.

A second issue concerns the development of a brand for the office that captures the public consciousness and asks whether the title 'ombudsman' might operate as a hindrance in this respect. The public profile of the office of PSO has always been an issue of some concern, with multiple studies suggesting a low awareness amongst citizens (Bondy and Doyle: 486–488). In this context, might the introduction of a new PSO scheme be an opportunity to re-publicise the office with a fresh title, one with a

[1] Company, Limited Liability Partnership and Business Names (Sensitive Words and Expressions) Regulations 2014.

better chance of generating popular recognition for the office? Change carries risks of confusion given the long-standing existence of PSOs in the UK and not all accept that the title 'ombudsman' is a significant barrier to awareness, but around the world numerous examples exist of alternative titles operating that do not appear to have undermined the office either. Some alternative examples include Public Rights Protector, Mediator, Public Defender, Public Complaints Commission, and the Commission for Administrative Justice.

We do not aim to resolve this debate in this book, but suggest that the new legislation should provide for a highly formal and neutral title, such as the 'Parliamentary Commissioner for Public Service Complaints', but thereafter allow room for the office itself to establish a brand as it sees fit, subject to reporting requirements. In practice, this is how PSO in the UK have proceeded in the past, such as with the current Parliamentary and Health Service Ombudsman (PHSO) which despite the labelling is formally an amalgamation of two statutory offices, the Parliamentary Commissioner for Administration (PCA) and the Health Service Commissioner for England. Likewise, the Local Government and Social Care Ombudsman (LGSCO) is formally the Commission for Local Administration in England.

The Book

In the chapters that follow, some of the UK's leading academics on the ombudsman draw together existing research and provide expert perspectives on the key themes that will need to underpin any new legislation for a new Parliamentary PSO.

Chapter 2 knits together the overall themes of the book into an overarching proposal for legislative reform. It charts a way forward, arguing that what is needed is the introduction of new legislation that not only fixes perceived current problems in the ombudsman sector, but is capable of providing the foundations for a successful office over several generations. This legislation should better equip the office to contribute towards the delivery of administrative justice by combining flexibility and ambition in the powers granted to the PSO, while constraining the office through well-constructed accountability devices and duties rather than unnecessary legislative prescription. The solution proposed is that legislative reform should be shaped by five core design principles. The following chapters provide more detailed (and sometimes more challenging) analysis of the issues underlying the five principles identified in this chapter.

In Chap. 3, Nick O'Brien advances a theoretical basis for the development of a PSO that is progressive and democratic. In so doing, the chapter seeks to answer the question of what sort of PSO we want and need. It offers a critical account of the apparent consensus on 'modern ombudsman practice', characterised by the prioritisation of the individual user, system, and dispute resolution. It associates 'modern ombudsman practice' of this sort with a jurisprudential mentality, with the values of the 'new public management', with the ideal of the quasi-judicial 'ombud' and its priorities of negative individual rights, boundaries, and adjudication. As an alternative, it proposes the democratic 'ombud' founded upon the 'demosprudential' values of community, human rights principle, and deliberative practice. It concludes that the demosprudential path is the necessary means of attaining 'the People's Ombud' and a PSO that is true to its democratic roots. This will require the acquisition by the PSO of different powers, as well as a willingness and capacity to use them.

In Chap. 4, Carolyn Hirst and Chris Gill consider the scope of the PSO's jurisdiction. On the one hand, the chapter argues for an integrated approach to English public services; on the other, it argues for reverting back to a stand-alone Parliamentary office for UK-wide public services. In reaching this conclusion, this chapter sets out seven principles for identifying the correct jurisdiction for a PSO. When assessed against these principles, the current draft Bill has a number of weaknesses: it fails to recognise the increasing blurring between public and private service provision; it does not recognise the need for the PSO jurisdiction to reflect the devolution settlement; it takes an unprincipled approach to integration; and it fails to consider how sensitivity to different service user needs can be maintained within an integrated PSO.

In Chap. 5, Chris Gill argues that a PSO should be granted own-initiative powers of investigation. The case for this is four-fold: the prevalence of these powers and successful experiences internationally; evidence in relation to complaining behaviour and the non-emergence of disputes; evidence in relation to under-representation of vulnerable groups; and identification of clear added-value contributions arising from own-initiative powers. The chapter explores how own-initiative powers should be calibrated and framed. International practice is analysed in relation to investigation triggers, criteria for launching investigations, and topics commonly investigated. The chapter considers three arguments against own-initiative powers—the 'red-tape', 'mission drift', and 'rogue ombudsman' arguments—and suggests that each of these can be answered through appropriate legislative framing. This chapter concludes that broad powers are required, controlled through reporting requirements that balance accountability and effectiveness.

In Chap. 6, Chris Gill contends that a PSO should be granted Complaint Standards Authority (CSA) powers. It begins by defining these powers, since they represent a recent innovation, confined to the devolved jurisdictions of the UK. The chapter then makes a case for the adoption of CSA powers, based on three arguments: evidence shows that problems within public service complaint systems are acute and urgent; the scale of these problems means that formal intervention is likely to be required; and the PSO is best placed in terms of expertise to address these issues. The chapter ends by considering arguments against CSA powers, and concludes that these can be mitigated, particularly if the vision of a more powerful and conceptually coherent ombudsman, recommended in this book, is accepted.

In Chap. 7, Naomi Creutzfeldt discusses the citizens' voice in an ombudsman process. She argues that a reformed PSO needs to have mechanisms in place to integrate users' views into the decision-making process. This will benefit citizens' experience of the complaint process and foster legitimacy and trust in the PSO institution. It will also help in educating the public about PSO's responsibilities. Taking users' views into account in the design and management of the PSO will assist in getting the best out of the system. Informed by empirical evidence, the chapter focuses on three topics: (1) procedural fairness; (2) managing expectations; and (3) systemic learning, data collection, and reporting. The chapter concludes with practical recommendations for an amended PSO legislation, which better integrates user-views.

In Chap. 8, Richard Kirkham identifies a range of legislative reform measures that will add clarity and refinement to the powers and procedural fairness of the ombudsman design. Some are relatively minor and uncontentious, others address flaws that have been identified in legal dispute. Not all were included in the 2016 draft Bill. This chapter also highlights how, as pressure on it has grown, the ombudsman sector has taken the initiative in devising new techniques to allow for enhanced accountability. These include measures to be more transparent in decision-making and to reconsider its decisions, and these new practices should now be made a duty in legislation. Finally, the chapter argues for the new legislation to be written in framework form wherever possible, to facilitate subsequent flexibility and amendment.

In Chap. 9, Brian Thompson explores the continuing challenge of holding to account an institution, the proposed PSO, which is itself a mechanism of accountability, while ensuring that its independence is not impaired. The model of Officers of Parliament, as developed in the UK and New Zealand, is used as the template for an examination of the provisions in the draft Bill. While these provisions draw heavily on the first official to be considered an Officer of Parliament, the Comptroller and Auditor General, there are variations relating to the arrangements for appointment and corporate governance. The conclusions recommend a wider debate on both (a) Officers of Parliament as a distinct unit of our constitutional watchdogs and (b) corporate governance which has not had the attention given to the accessibility, role, and powers of the PSO, as well as suggesting specific changes to the draft legislative provisions.

References

Abraham, A. (2008). The Ombudsman as Part of the UK Constitution: A Contested Role? *Parliamentary Affairs, 61*, 206–215.

Bondy, V., & Doyle, M. (2018). What's in a Name: A Discussion Paper on Ombud Terminology. In M. Hertogh & R. Kirkham (Eds.), *Research Handbook on the Ombudsman*. Cheltenham: Edward Elgar.

Cabinet Office. (2000). *Review of the Public Sector Ombudsmen in England*. London: Cabinet Office.

Cabinet Office. (2016). *Draft Public Service Ombudsman Bill*. Cm. 9374.

Gordon, R. (2013). *Governance of Local Government Ombudsman Service: A report for the Secretary of State for Communities and Local Government*. London: Department for Communities and Local Government.

Gordon, R. (2014). *Better to Serve the Public: Proposals to Restructure, Reform, Renew and Reinvigorate Public Services Ombudsmen*. London: Cabinet Office.

Gregory, R., & Giddings, P. (2002). *The Ombudsman, the Citizen and Parliament*. London: Politicos Publishing.

Jersey Law Commission. (2018). *Designing a Public Services Ombudsman for Jersey*. Retrieved November 7, 2019, from https://jerseylawcommission.files.wordpress.com/2018/11/jsylawcom_designingombudsman_final.pdf.

Kirkham, R. (2007). *The Parliamentary Ombudsman: Withstanding the test of time, in Fourth Report of the Parliamentary Commissioner for Administration, The Parliamentary Ombudsman: Withstanding the test of time*, HC 421 (2006–07).

Kirkham, R. (2017). *Challenging the Ombudsman: Are Review Processes Adequate?* Retrieved November 27, 2019, from https://www.nuffieldfoundation.org/challenging-ombudsman-are-review-processes-adequate.

Kirkham, R., & Martin, J. (2014). Designing an English Public Services Ombudsman. *Journal of Social Welfare and Family Law, 36*(3), 330–348.

Kirkham, R., & Thompson, B. (2017). *An Initial Commentary on the Draft Public Services Ombuds Bill.* Retrieved November 25, 2019, from https://ukaji.org/2016/12/20/an-initial-commentary-on-the-draft-public-services-ombuds-bill/.

Law Commission. (2011). (Law Com No 329) *Public Services Ombudsmen* HC 1136.

McBurnie, G. (2017). *The Draft Public Service Ombudsman Bill: What Recommendations Are Being Taken Forward?* Retrieved November 25, 2019, from https://ukaji.org/2017/01/12/the-draft-public-service-ombudsman-bill-what-recommendations-are-being-taken-forward/.

McMillan, J. (2008, April 22). *What's in a Name? Use of the Term 'Ombudsman'*, Commonwealth Ombudsman. Presentation to the Australian and New Zealand Ombudsman Association, Melbourne.

Northern Ireland Assembly. (2015, April 20). Public Services Ombudsperson Bill, Explanatory and Financial Memorandum. Retrieved November 25, 2019, from http://www.niassembly.gov.uk/globalassets/documents/legislation/bills/non-executive-bills/session-2015-2016/public-services-ombudsperson-bill/efm%2D%2D-as-introduced.pdf.

O'Brien, N. (2019). *No End of Searching: A Comment on the Draft Public Service Ombudsman Bill 2016.* Retrieved November 25, 2019, from https://ukaji.org/2017/02/02/no-end-of-searching-a-comment-on-the-draft-public-service-ombudsman-bill-2016/.

Ombudsman Association. (2019). *Criteria for the Recognition of Ombudsman Offices.* Retrieved October 31, 2019, from http://www.ombudsmanassociation.org/docs/OA-TermsandRulesJuly2019.pdf.

PASC (Public Administration Select Committee). (2007). *When Citizens Complain.* (2007–2008) HC 409.

PASC (Public Administration Select Committee). (2013–2014). Time for a People's Ombudsman Service. HC 655.

Reynolds, D. (2017). *A Service User Perspective of the Draft Legislation for the New Public Service Ombudsman.* Retrieved November 25, 2019, from https://ukaji.org/2017/01/26/a-service-user-perspective-of-the-draft-legislation-for-the-new-public-service-ombudsman/.

Whyatt, J. (1961). *The Citizen and the Administration: The Redress of Grievances.* London: Justice.

CHAPTER 2

Five Principles for a New Public Services Ombudsman

Richard Kirkham and Chris Gill

Abstract This chapter sets out five principles that should underpin the creation of a new Public Services Ombudsman (PSO). Principle 1 is that the new PSO must have a bolder role in the administrative justice system. Principle 2 is that there should be a presumption for the PSO having an integrated jurisdiction over all English public services, while respecting the UK's devolution settlement. Principle 3 is that the PSO must have a broad range of powers, reflective of those granted to PSOs in other jurisdictions. Principle 4 is that the new PSO must report on how it engages with citizens and on the delivery of administrative justice. Finally, Principle 5 is that the PSO must be subject to multiple accountability routes to ensure that a bolder role and new powers are used appropriately. These principles address the principal controversies which face legislators in creating a new PSO and are designed to provide a guide to legislative reform.

R. Kirkham
Sheffield University, Sheffield, UK
e-mail: r.m.kirkham@sheffield.ac.uk

C. Gill (✉)
University of Glasgow, Glasgow, UK
e-mail: Chris.Gill@glasgow.ac.uk

R. Kirkham, C. Gill (eds.), *A Manifesto for Ombudsman Reform*,
https://doi.org/10.1007/978-3-030-40612-7_2

Keyword Legislative reform • Public Services Ombudsman • Administrative justice • Powers • Institutional design

This chapter sets out five principles which are designed to guide the creation of a new Public Services Ombudsman (PSO). The principles aim not only to fix perceived current problems (see Chap. 1), but to provide the foundations for a successful office over several generations. Overall, the principles seek to bolster the PSO's contribution to administrative justice by granting the office new powers and the ability to use these flexibly, while constraining the office through well-constructed accountability devices and duties. Each principle broadly reflects arguments made in subsequent chapters of this book, albeit that in some instances individual chapters go further by providing additional reform options for policymakers to consider. The table below sets out the principles which are discussed in this chapter and shows where the principles are followed through in subsequent chapters of the book.

Alongside these five principles, drafters of any new PSO legislation will need to take heed of additional foundational design concepts relating to the institution. These foundational concepts are already well established, for example, in the Council of Europe's *Venice Principles on the Protection and Promotion of the Ombudsman Institution* (Council of Europe 2019) and the Ombudsman Association's *Criteria for Membership* (Ombudsman Association 2019). On these foundational concepts, such as a PSO's need for independence or the right to unhindered access to the PSO, we take it for granted that they must underpin legislative reform and accept that the draft Public Services Ombudsman Bill ('the draft Bill': Cabinet Office 2016) represents a very strong starting point. As a result, in this chapter, we do not consider these foundational issues any further. Instead, the five principles laid out here focus on key areas where controversies remain and where reform is needed that requires resolution through legislating for a new PSO (Table 2.1).

Table 2.1 The five principles for reform as developed in later chapters

Principle for legislative reform	*Chapter in which issues covered*
1. The PSO should have a bolder role within the administrative justice system	Chapter 3 (Nick O'Brien)
2. There should be a presumption in favour of the PSO having jurisdiction over all English public services, while respecting the UK's devolution settlement	Chapter 4 (Carolyn Hirst and Chris Gill)
3. The PSO should possess a broad toolkit of powers	Chapters 5 and 6 (Chris Gill)
4. The PSO should be subject to a duty to report on engagement with citizens and delivery of administrative justice	Chapter 7 (Naomi Creutzfeldt)
5. The PSO should be subject to a range of accountability routes	Chapter 8 (Richard Kirkham) and Chapter 9 (Brian Thompson)

Principle 1: The PSO Should Have a Bolder Role in the Administrative Justice System

The Ombudsman's Contested Role

A long-standing debate in relation to PSOs has been what the role of the institution should be: is it primarily to settle individual complaints brought by citizens or is it instead to improve the quality of public administration at large? These roles have been referred to respectively as 'fire-fighting' and 'fire-watching' (Harlow and Rawlings 2009), 'redress' and 'control' (Heede 2003), and 'fly swatting' and 'lion taming' (Harlow 2018). While normative arguments continue about which of these roles should be given priority, the reality is that PSOs are generally expected to perform both roles with variation relating to the exact balance achieved between the two. While this is the case, current PSO legislation in the UK fails to articulate clearly what roles the PSO is expected to fulfil and, to the extent a role is articulated, the focus has tended to be on emphasising the PSO's role as a complaint handler. This has been unhelpful and has allowed misunderstandings to arise about what the PSO is and should be doing among policymakers, providers of public services, and citizens.

While the current emphasis on complaint-handling is important (see Chap. 7 by Naomi Creutzfeldt), the lack of concern with the PSO's broader and potentially more transformative role can be seen as reductive (see Chap. 3 by Nick O'Brien). Several recent examples of systemic maladministration within government, such as the Windrush affair, in which the Parliamentary and Health Services Ombudsman (PHSO) played no role, serve to highlight why failing to recognise a broader role for the PSO is problematic. Here, there is significant evidence that systemic maladministration took place within the Home Office in its handling of the immigration status of multiple UK citizens that arrived in the UK from the 1940s onwards, with the result that hundreds of people experienced hardship (Home Affairs Committee 2018). Given that the first information about the possibility of maladministration became public knowledge some time before the Home Office finally accepted responsibility, would it not have been preferable for the PHSO to have been able to intervene at an early stage regardless of whether a complaint had made its way through the system or not? This is the approach adopted in most other countries, but was difficult for the PHSO to undertake because of lack of powers to conduct investigations without being first in receipt of a complaint (see Chap. 5 by Chris Gill). A similar tale of under-scrutiny of public administration may be told about ongoing grievances with regard to the Universal Credit scheme (Work and Pensions Committee 2018) and the registration of EU citizens (Tomlinson 2019) and hints at a regulatory space in the administrative justice system which the PSO could fill.

Recognising Multiple Roles in Statute

Thus, we propose that legislation should contain a clear statement of the multiple roles that the PSO is expected to fulfil. This will provide clarity for Parliament, government, and citizens about the multi-dimensional nature of the PSO and will help to avoid incorrect claims from stakeholders that the office is either overreaching or failing to fulfil its purpose. Thereafter, the office, and its overseers, should be entrusted with the responsibility for making good use of that set of powers. The onus should be on a bottom-up approach to deciding the optimum balance of roles for the office. This solution allows the PSO, and Parliament through its oversight select committees, to vary the emphasis of the office to respond to changes over time, while recognising that the PSO is more than a complaint handler and, instead, has a bolder and more far-reaching role to play within the administrative justice system. This bolder role needs to be supported in various ways (such as through the provision of new powers as discussed in Principle 3 below), but at the outset the legislation should clearly set out the objects which a PSO is expected to fulfil. A good example of how this might be done can be found in the following provision from the Ombudsman Act (Queensland) 2001 s.5:

The objects of this Act are—

(a) to give people a timely, effective, independent and just way of having administrative actions of agencies investigated; and
(b) to improve the quality of decision-making and administrative practice in agencies.

The provision might be adapted further:

(c) to address instances of systemic maladministration in public service; and
(d) to create trust in public administration and accountability of public bodies.

We do not propose that legislation should be used to settle the degree of priority that each of these roles should be afforded. Flexibility should be ensured so that individual office holders and future Parliaments can decide where the exact emphasis between the roles should fall. However, a major problem facing current PSOs is that they are essentially reactive and have limited tools available to prioritise different aspects of their work. In order to allow the new PSO to prioritise its work, and in recognition of the need to deploy limited resources in a way that can achieve the most benefit, legislation should allow the PSO to consider the public interest when deciding whether to investigate a complaint. This would allow the PSO, for example, to choose not to investigate complaints that do not meet a particular threshold of injustice or that appear to be confined to individual issues rather than raising issues of public concern. The granting of such filtering powers would allow the PSO to manage the number and nature of complaints it investigates and allow the office to determine the optimum balance between its various roles. To monitor how such choices are managed, this 'filtering function' is one of the aspects of the PSO's work which should be reported on and scrutinised on a regular basis (see Principles 4 and 5 below). While the vision of a demosprudential PSO advocated by O'Brien in Chap. 3 cannot be fully reflected in legislative provisions, making sure that legislation sets out a range of broader goals for the office and filtering mechanisms that give the PSO the ability to vary the degree of emphasis on individual complaint-handling, provides a foundation on which a bolder role can be built for the PSO.

Preserving the Parliamentary Nature of the PSO

Finally, a feature of the PSO that should be re-emphasised in the reform process is the Parliamentary nature of the office and the fundamental role it has to play as an institution of democratic governance, which can contribute to processes of deliberative democracy (see O'Brien in Chap. 3). This would recognise that there has been a significant shift since 1967 in the way in which the office operates as a 'parliamentary ombudsman'. The original vision was that the office would be a 'cutting edge' (Drewry and Harlow 1990) for MPs to use in resolving their more complex and intractable constituency casework. The office was to be an additional tool in Parliament and MPs' complaint-handling machinery. In terms of the next phase of the office's development, the Parliamentary nature of the role should be conceived more in terms of providing Parliament with assistance in the business of scrutinising and holding government to account. As a result, we propose that the office should continue to operate as an Officer of Parliament and this designation should be reflected in statute (see Chap. 9 by Brian Thompson). The PSO should be a cornerstone of the administrative justice system, with a particular duty to operate as a scrutiniser of public administration and public services. In fulfilling this task it should be seen to provide a service for the benefit of the legislature, which is the ultimate guarantor of public administration, as well as the individual citizen.

Principle 2: There Should Be a Presumption in Favour of the PSO Having Jurisdiction Over All English Public Services, While Respecting the UK's Devolution Settlement

A Statutory Requirement to Provide Reasons for Establishing a Function-Specific PSO Office

The current PSO landscape in England is a complex patchwork of bespoke and function-specific offices, with eight separate PSO offices (see Chap. 4:

Table 4.1). Following the example of the UK's devolved nations, we suggest that the starting presumption should be that all aspects of public service are integrated into a single office unless there is a good reason for establishing a bespoke office (see Chap. 4 by Carolyn Hirst and Chris Gill). This approach minimises the potential for complexity in managing multi-faceted complaints that crossover the functions of different public bodies and for confusion from the perspective of the citizen. A single-office model also offers potential to increase the public recognition of the institution, which has generally been lacking in England. Chapter 4 of this book provides a more detailed discussion of the question of jurisdiction, including specific recommendations for legislative reform, but a number of important issues are covered here.

First, there may be pragmatic and organisational reasons for not being overly ambitious with the initial wave of harmonisation that accompanies the introduction of the new PSO, as with the draft Bill which confined its remit to four existing jurisdictions (central government, health, local government, and social care), plus the potential for a fifth (housing). However, although we make no specific recommendations on the extent to which harmonisation should be extended, we do suggest that administrative and sector convenience is not a good reason by itself to exclude the integration of other current schemes into the PSO. Therefore, in the future, all new jurisdictions in the public sector should be considered for integration, including sectors such as housing and higher education that are currently located in separate specialised offices. To maximise the potential for a powerful and simply organised PSO, this presumption in favour of the single-office model should be stated in the PSO Bill.[1] In addition, it should be a legislative requirement for the government to provide reasons for establishing a new bespoke PSO rather than integrating the function into the single-office model. An integrated PSO on the lines suggested here would complement the reforms of the tribunal service in the Tribunals, Courts, and Enforcement Act 2007 and be a further step towards adding coherence and clarity to the UK's administrative justice system.

[1] There will be certain areas of public service from which a PSO's investigative remit should be excluded, such as for reasons of national security, or because they are considered to belong in the legal domain only, such as with the commencement and operation of legal proceedings or contractual and employment disputes. However, such exclusions should be limited and specified on the face of the new PSO legislation.

Ensuring Jurisdiction Over Privately Delivered Public Goods and Public Interest Services

A further principle that should be embedded in legislation is an acknowledgement of the changing landscape for public service delivery and the increasing involvement of the private sector. As a starting point, the rationale for integrating a particular service into the PSO should be the degree of public interest inherent in the function concerned. Perhaps the clearest rationale for not integrating a function into the PSO is in the consumer sector, where it is unclear why the public purse should be used to support quality control if a viable alternative is available. However, the boundary line of the appropriate remit of the PSO is uncertain. For instance, the public interest in public transport is sufficiently strong that this sector should be considered for inclusion in the PSO's jurisdiction notwithstanding the private ownership model that dominates here. Similar arguments might be made in relation to other essential services, such as energy.

Less controversially, the existing principle that the PSOs' remits should 'follow the money' if a public service provider chooses to contract out provision to a private provider should be confirmed and clearly spelled out in new legislation (Gordon 2014: paras. 73–77). Unless specifically provided for by legislation, it should not be possible to contract out of the right to administrative justice through the PSO. An additional scenario is that covered by the Public Services Ombudsman (Wales) Act 2019 which has created a new power (s.16) for the Welsh PSO to investigate certain complaints about the private provision of health services. This provision is designed to optimise the capacity for the PSO to review complaints which in origin concern publicly funded healthcare, but which 'cannot be investigated effectively or completely without also investigating [a private] health-related service' (Public Services Ombudsman (Wales) Act 2019: s.16(2)). A similar power should be considered in England. Likewise, legislation in England has clarified that social care services provided by private bodies should come under the remit of the Local Government and Social Care Ombudsman (LGSCO) (Health Act 2009: s.35, sch.5). The same approach needs to be adopted for other private bodies that are clearly providing public goods, as with school academies (Education Committee 2019: paras. 31–32) or social housing. Against private sector providers at least, consideration should be given to granting the PSO the power to seek judicial enforcement of recommendations and recover the costs of investigating complaints about non-public bodies from the providers themselves.

Arguments That Would Justify the Creation of Stand-Alone PSOs

As noted above, the legislation should impose a duty on government to give reasons where a decision is taken to create a new stand-alone PSO rather than integrating a new jurisdiction into the single-office PSO. What would constitute good reasons for doing this? As Hirst and Gill argue in Chap. 3, three factors are relevant here:

- the degree of controversy attached to the jurisdiction;
- the seriousness of the issues arising in the jurisdiction; and
- the level of public interest involved.

Thus, there may be something in the nature of the remit that requires a specialist PSO or other perceived benefits in ring-fencing the relevant public service. Here a key concern is the political sensitivity and/or distinct nature of the service in question. Hence, the functions of the police, prisons, and armed services are dealt with by a specialised body in several countries. One important factor here is the need to retain the confidence of the sector being overseen, which might entail building a specialised office with distinct features. It might also be thought that on occasion the nature of a PSO's specialist input is inappropriate or that another body/approach could achieve better results. For instance, the 2017–2019 Conservative Government's introduction of a new Health Service Safety Investigation Body (HSSIB) can be seen in this light (Department of Health 2017). Following a steady series of major incidents in the National Health Service (NHS) that raised serious safety concerns, the government chose to introduce a body with more specialised knowledge to investigate and understand local incidents and improve standards.

The Organisational Structure of the PSO

An integrated PSO, covering more public services and dealing with more complaints, will require an organisational structure that allows it to give attention to sector-specific issues, at the same time as providing a single point of entry for citizens and allowing for cross-cutting investigations and learning throughout public services. The approach which we recommend is the adoption of a 'collegiate' structure, as recommended in the 2000 Cabinet Office Report (Cabinet Office 2000: ch.5). A 'collegiate' body made up of multiple office holders was an idea specifically rejected by Gordon in his 2014 review on the basis that it might 'detract from the status and authority of the chief office holder' (2014: paras. 110–113). This arrangement might also facilitate rivalries between individual office holders or encourage an expectation in particular sectors that they had a nominated point of influence within the PSO.

But the new PSO legislation could instead establish a less rigid internal collegiate structure. First, a power to appoint sectoral lead PSO might be created, but that power would be a permissive one wielded by the chief office holder as appropriate. This would create an expectation that individual sectors would be recognised within the PSO, but place the roles clearly at the discretion of the chief office holder. These sectoral lead PSOs would lead on sector complaint-handling and spearhead efforts to improve administration in the sector concerned, but be directly accountable to the chief office holder. Likewise, the new integrated PSO could be required to report separately on listed jurisdictions within its annual report. Although the chief office holder would retain final responsibility for all decisions and internally the organisation would operate as a single entity, functionally the individual jurisdictions would thereby remain strongly recognised.

This reporting requirement, and associated structure, would still enable a single point of entry for all complaints and allow the office to organise single investigations for complaints that crossover sectorial boundaries. It would also have two significant advantages. First, it would not only pay formal recognition to the individual sectors incorporated into the PSO, but it would allow for a clearer separation of the role of the chief office holder from day-to-day complaint-handling. This might facilitate the adoption of a more natural and quasi-autonomous internal review process for individual complaints, whereby the chief office holder would be responsible for considering reviews from the sectoral leads and overseeing internal quality control processes. Second, it might provide the framework for one solution to the devolution problem which we turn to next.

Respecting the UK's Devolution Settlement

One of the reasons given for the failure of the 2000 Cabinet Office recommendation to establish an integrated PSO in the UK was the difficulty of dealing with the implications of devolution. Even after the establishment of separate schemes in the devolved nations, the UK-wide PCA (Parliamentary Commissioner for Administration) office is still responsible for receiving complaints about central government departments from citizens living outside England. The number of such complaints resolved by the PCA is relatively small,[2] but the symbolism of a predominantly English office being empowered to resolve the complaints of residents living outside England would contradict the devolution settlement (see Elliott 2006 and Chap. 4) and possibly create political resentment. There are a number of different options that might be considered to address this, all of which have drawbacks.[3] Our preferred option, and that which is advanced in Chap. 4, is for the retention of a separate PSO to cover UK-wide public services. While this may appear to contradict the general principle around integration, a separate office is fully justified in order to reflect accurately the UK's territorial constitution.[4]

Principle 3: The PSO Should Possess a Broad Toolkit of Powers

The Toolkit

Principle 1 above suggested that the Parliamentary PSO should be viewed as a powerful administrative justice institution, fulfilling multiple roles, but particularly moving beyond a sole emphasis on individual complaint-handling in order to pursue bolder goals around realising good administration, trust, and accountability in government. Even with the existence in the system of other institutions of government oversight, such as auditors, other complaint-handling bodies, and regulators, the PSO has a distinct contribution to offer. The PSO's emphasis on administrative fairness and good administration (rather than administrative efficiency or compliance with regulatory or professional standards) provides it with a unique locus

[2] Gordon recorded it as 10% of the PCA workload (Gordon 2014: 115).

[3] For example, retain a separate PCA office for investigating complaints from residents living outside England only and appoint an existing UK officer, for instance the Parliamentary Commissioner for Standards, as responsible ombudsman. Alternatively, delegate investigation to the relevant devolved PSOs depending on the residence of the complainant.

[4] The risk is that, as with the current office of the PHSO, the temptation would be to appoint the new, and predominantly English PSO office, as the PCA and 'administratively' to merge the two schemes together, thus rendering the separation symbolic only. But the retention of a separate PCA would remain symbolically important and stipulate a separate reporting duty on the office for any pan-UK (or partially pan-UK) central government function.

of action that complements other oversight mechanisms. A broad emphasis on securing good administration would also allow the PSO to fill gaps in the system of public scrutiny, as well as report on any failures in the system of scrutiny itself. To do this and to deliver on its promise, the PSO needs to be equipped with new powers. Some of the required powers are well-provided for in existing legislation, particularly in terms of investigatory and reporting powers. However, new powers will be required in three areas.

First, as is outlined in Chap. 8 by Richard Kirkham, there are multiple technical issues that require attention as the legislation has become dated over time, such as with complaint processes and reporting powers. For instance, a major limitation of the 1967 legislation was that it conceived of formal investigation and reporting as the only means of handling grievances, yet developments in complaint-handling and citizen expectations have led to quicker, less formal, more consensual approaches. In recognition of such developments, the legislation should avoid being overly prescriptive on questions of process and practice, allowing the PSO as much discretion as possible to meet the demands of the multiple roles it is required to play. Updating these powers should not be a difficult task, and indeed was partially addressed in the draft Bill. As the PSO model has now been adopted around the world, especially in common law countries, there are several very good legislative examples to copy from, not least in the devolved nations.

Second, there is a need to respond to specific problems that have been identified over time in caselaw. A steady flow of judicial review cases have now been considered by the courts, which have led to the identification of several narrow, but nonetheless important, legal uncertainties. The solutions provided by the courts should be considered and in the main reflected in the way that the PSO's powers are refined. Some of these points are listed in Chap. 8. For instance, in order to make it easier for the PSO to investigate maladministration, the office should be empowered to expand an investigation beyond a complaint if it is in the public interest to do so. The PSO should also be empowered to quash its own decisions if it subsequently identifies errors in its decision-making and the power to make recommendations, including recommendations for financial compensation, should be clarified.[5] Finally, in recognition of the potential for the PSO to

[5] Ambiguity around this matter was at issue in Supreme Court case of *JR55* [2016] UKSC 22.

come across legal anomalies, both in its own jurisdiction and the powers of public authority more generally, the office should be given a power to refer legal questions to the courts. This might include the power to challenge authorities that fail to follow the correct process in responding to PSO reports.

A third area where the PSO's powers need to be strengthened is more ambitious and goes direct to the argument that consideration needs to be given as to how to maximise the potential of the office. There is a broad consensus that the 'English' legislative approach to the office is the most restrictive in the world (e.g. Buck et al. 2011). Elsewhere, including in the common law world, the PSO model has been modernised and enhanced to a much larger degree. This context means that the drafters of the proposed new PSO legislation will be spoilt for choice as to ideas for reform given the broad, extended, and global use of the ombudsman model across both public and private sectors. The range of legislative alternatives and the experience of their operation provide rich pickings and comparative lessons in the art of how to do, and not to do, legislative design. The two most commonly cited examples of extra powers are the power to launch an investigation of the office's own initiative and without waiting for a complaint to be submitted,[6] and a set of powers that allow it to operate as a complaint standards authority with a brief to regulate the quality of complaint-handling offered by public service providers.

The first of these powers expands the capacity of the PSO to intervene when there are prima facie indications of maladministration (see Chap. 5 by Chris Gill). The Parliamentary PSO could be notified by a range of sources—for example, Parliamentarians, whistle-blowers, media reports, public authorities—of the existence of serious concerns with the administrative quality of service being provided by a public body. For instance, as noted above, such a power would have sanctioned PHSO to intervene in cases such as the Windrush Affair where no complaints were made to the PHSO's office (Home Affairs Committee 2018). Alternatively, a PSO might of its own volition and on the back of its own research surmise that there is a public interest reason to investigate a public service, perhaps because of multiple complaints in a single area or the reverse, a surprising

[6] There is a range of terminology used to describe this power, for example own motion, own initiative, ex officio investigations. It is not clear that this terminology is particularly helpful and legislators may wish to consider alternatives for describing these powers such as 'public interest investigations'.

absence of complaints from potentially vulnerable citizens. This power should be limited by providing for suitable consultation and notification requirements prior to a public interest investigation being launched. For example, the PSO should be under a duty to consult relevant oversight bodies before deciding on whether to pursue an investigation.

The second set of powers relates to the provision of quasi-regulatory responsibilities in relation to the system for public service complaint-handling (see Chap. 6 by Chris Gill). The concept is controversial insofar as it raises the prospect of the office drifting away from its role as a complaint handler and in the sense that it changes the methodology of the office from one of investigation to one involving the regulatory activities of standard-setting, monitoring, and compliance checking. However, the logical strength in the PSO's office using its knowledge to promote good complaint-handling is that, by virtue of its core complaint-handling function, it is as well placed as any institution to monitor or track current standards of complaint-handling being applied by service providers and collate best practice in the sector.

Collectively, these new powers connect most closely to what O'Brien in his chapter in this collection refers to as demosprudence (see Chap. 3). In other words, while the exact balance to be reached between the PSO's complaint-handling and broader systemic functions should be subject to flexible adaptation over time, the true capacity of the office to make a difference to government administration rests 'on the willingness and capacity to use [its] powers to develop different types of relationship with the legislature and the judiciary, and critically with the People' (Chap. 3: 52). Providing the PSO with Complaint Standards Authority powers should allow the PSO to devote more time to the most egregious complaints of maladministration, in the knowledge that appropriate mechanisms exist to deal with the vast majority of less serious matters. The own initiative power of investigation meanwhile would allow the PSO to engage in investigations that provide opportunities for genuine reflection on the requirements of good administration and open up deliberative spaces for citizens, public service providers, and Parliamentarians to consider where improvements in administration are required.

The objection to the granting of such broader powers is ordinarily based on the fear of ombudsman overreach, the risk that a PSO might be distracted from complaint-handling, and the potential added exposure to reputational pressure and damage in how those powers are used. Whilst real and present dangers, these risks are probably overstated and there is little evidence that in general this fear has been realised in those offices that already possess such powers. Further, to the extent that there is a risk they can be addressed through consultation and reporting duties, as well as general oversight, rather than legislative control.

Allowing Space for Future Evolution

A challenge with the new legislation is that it will have to combine prescription and statutory direction in relation to core features of the PSO. There may be legislative temptation to attempt to confine the new office's discretion through law. This should be resisted for two reasons, first the inherent uncertainties in the nature of the PSO's powers and second the difficulties that would arise should subsequent amendments to legislation be required. As the history of the office demonstrates, the PSO is but one player in the administrative justice system and one that often operates outside the public eye. A consequence of this has been that it has proved difficult to find the time to reform the office, even when the government has largely been in favour of new measures. This practical inertia against reform should be recognised in the drafting of the legislation.

- First, the powers of the PSO should be drawn as widely as possible to allow for practice to adjust in the future.
- Second, the drafting of the PSO legislation should avoid excessive prescription and be written in framework form.

Of course, a general concern with wide-ranging discretionary power is that as well as allowing for positive innovation and adaptation over time, it creates room for unwanted use of that power, or in this instance the potential for a PSO to 'go rogue'. Here we advocate that the correct response is not to attempt to control for that risk through statutory prescription, but to build into the new scheme clear reporting duties and appropriate and sufficiently powerful accountability routes to discourage and identify any subsequent unwanted uses of discretionary power. Not only do such reporting duties encourage transparency, but experiments in the use of the office's powers can be tested through experience and an ongoing dialogue with Parliament and other stakeholders.

Principle 4: The PSO Should Be Subject to a Duty to Report on Engagement with Citizens and the Delivery of Administrative Justice

Duties and Accountability

The solution to safeguarding against the misuse of the expanded powers and broader role for the ombudsman we have recommended will be to ensure robust accountability arrangements. To facilitate this process, the new legislation should map out a clear list of duties that the PSO should be required to report on. This list will go further than the relatively undefined reporting duties on the office at present. The significance of this approach is that it will chart the expectations of the office as of now (more duties can be added if and when new expectations are made of the office), but will leave it to the PSO to select and adapt the most appropriate approach with which to fulfil the duty. The PSO, therefore, as the authority best placed to make judgements on effective strategies and choices, is left to manage public resources across its range of duties, but an obligation to transparency both of stated strategies and of delivery will render the office regularly accountable for those choices.

Engagement with Citizens

A key stakeholder for the PSO is the citizen. It is important to be clear here that by citizens, we do not only mean those who have used the office (complainants) but all members of the public who are likely to benefit from the existence of a body focused on righting injustices, improving public administration, and helping Parliament hold government to account. By way of recognising the importance of this aspect of the PSO's work, the office should be required to report annually on its engagement with complainants and citizens across a range of measures, including details on:

- Policy and guidance on decision-making standards applied
- Operational performance standards
- Decisions made
- Internal review processes on decision and service complaints
- Consultations with complainants and citizens
- Public engagement work with citizens

- Efforts to publicise the office to vulnerable citizens
- Advisory forums
- Profile of complainants

Chapter 7 of this book by Naomi Creutzfeldt highlights the main reasons why communication with users is vital to the success of the institution, with three reasons standing out: the need to demonstrate procedural fairness towards individual complainants; the demand for transparency about decisions and decision-making criteria being applied; and the value in integrating the views of citizens into the design of the ombudsman's processes.

Procedural Fairness

The concept of procedural fairness underpins all dispute resolution processes deployed in the justice system. As one of a PSO's functions is to investigate complaints and there is a widespread expectation that such work will lead to redress where appropriate, the demand for high standards of procedural fairness is unavoidable. The long-term credibility of the office will always be in part based upon the quality of the service that it provides for users. This standard can in part be met by legal safeguards, but the PSO's ongoing capacity and performance in delivering procedural fairness needs to be reported upon and scrutinised. Given the profound difficulties in challenging ombudsman decisions in the courts, the goal of procedural fairness must necessarily include offering, and being fully transparent about, opportunities for individual decisions and the quality of service to be challenged (see Chap. 7) as the Ombudsman Association's (OA's) membership criteria stipulates (Ombudsman Association 2019: rule 3 'effectiveness'). A similar duty to give guidance should also apply for how the office interprets its legal grounds for finding administrative fault: namely, maladministration, service failure, and injustice. Efforts to define in detail such concepts in law will always leave gaps in detail (Jersey Law Commission 2018: ch.8), but placing the burden on the PSO to explain its understanding of administrative fault offers the potential for greater explanation and occasional updates. Finally, although the detail should be left for the PSO to organise, the office should be under a statutory duty to operate both a decision and a service review process and be required to report on the throughput and outcomes of cases considered.

Transparency
For confidence and awareness of the office to be maintained, all stakeholders, not just individual or potential complainants, need to have access to knowledge about the decisions that are made by the PSO. The importance of transparency is accepted by much of the ombudsman sector and has become a feature of recent best practice but this policy needs to become an in-built statutory duty. Thus the PSO should be obliged to publish details of the decision-making criteria that it relies upon and publish every decision in full, subject to discretionary safeguards to protect anonymity.

Consulting with Citizens
A further aspect of a PSO's duty towards the citizen has not always received full attention, and that is the benefits of good communication with both current complainants and citizens more generally. One particular challenge here is to manage complainant expectations of the service provided by a PSO. This ideally is a front-loaded process, but will require in-built opportunities to challenge decisions and services provided.

Additionally however, the ongoing management of the PSO requires the integration of the citizen's perspective in order to best deliver a service that caters for the needs of all potential complainants, including vulnerable users. This is not just a matter of working with individual existing complainants, but finding ways to include the perspectives of citizens in the background policy-making and quality control processes. A key issue here is to challenge a PSO to consider whether it is reaching out sufficiently to all potential complainants, with a perennial concern in the sector that PSOs tend to favour citizens already well-equipped to protect their interests leaving vulnerable groups disadvantaged (Hubeau 2018). Advisory forums and consultation processes are common techniques to achieve this form of communication and collation of citizen knowledge. In keeping with O'Brien's argument (Chap. 3) about the development of a demosprudential approach, citizens and citizens' needs should be placed at the heart of the PSO's work. This would involve using mechanisms such as consultation and co-production to deliver in practice the PSO's potential to act as a bridging agent between citizens and the state. Again, the existence and effectiveness of such processes need to be reported upon.

Promotion of Administrative Justice

PSOs possess a range of reporting duties that go beyond individual investigations. Thus they report annually on their performance and often can issue additional 'special' reports in the public interest. We suggest though that the reporting remit of the PSO should include an overall duty to report annually on its contribution towards administrative justice, a duty which should be broken down into a series of sub-demands. For instance, the following list of features of the PSO's work should be addressed:

- Quality control of standards of decision-making
- Implementation of recommendations
- Analysis of PSO complaints per sector
- Engagement with bodies in jurisdiction
- Results of systemic and public interest investigations
- Implementation of the Complaint Standards Authority role
- Details of any legal developments affecting the PSO (including all proceedings brought by way of judicial review, Freedom of Information claims, etc.)
- Consultations with other oversight bodies
- A statement on the administrative justice system
- Periodic independent and peer review

As with other reporting duties, the nature of the solutions chosen by the PSO to demonstrate that it has met its duties should be left to an ongoing conversation between the office holder, the Board, and Parliament. However, the following brief comments will be made here.

The importance of evidencing that the office delivers high standards of administrative justice has already been commented upon above. The additional point being made here is that the PSO needs to demonstrate on a regular basis that it is reflecting on those standards and setting them appropriately. A requirement to set up an independent quality assurance board and to publish all decisions and policy criteria would make this set of reporting duties easier to fulfil (see Chap. 8). Additionally, a major claim made in favour of the PSO is that it can promote good administration in the longer term. The reporting duties listed above are designed to force the PSO to demonstrate how these goals are delivered upon and to what extent they are effective.

Other reporting duties, however, should go beyond the detail of the PSO's performance and reflect upon the various interconnections between the office and other administrative justice institutions. The concern raised sometimes that the PSO might duplicate the work of other watchdogs (Cabinet Office 2015: 16) is best rebutted by identifying how the office liaises with other institutions to avoid and manage such overlaps. Such consultations should become a required part of the process of setting-up own-initiative investigations but need to go further. Indeed, given the PSO's wide brief in terms of remit and powers, it will be ideally situated to play a leadership role in acting as a voice for the administrative justice system as a whole and reporting on any gaps in provision that it has observed or problems of accessibility to justice. As part of this role, the PSO might have a duty to report to Parliament on all refusals of public service providers to implement recommendations made by complaints handlers.

Finally, the new PSO should build on the triennial review model currently included in the LGSCO legislation. Whereas this model establishes a three year internally led exercise, in the future the office should be required on a periodic basis to commission an independent review (e.g. once every seven years) of the organisation and its statute, and report to Parliament its findings. An alternative model would be for that commissioning duty to fall upon a Parliamentary select committee.

Principle 5: The PSO Should Be Subject to a Range of Accountability Routes

There are risks in conferring wide powers on any administrative body, which increase with a body such as a PSO given that it necessarily operates with considerable autonomy from direct democratic oversight. The potential for 'overreach' is real. PSOs already make numerous decisions that impact citizens, absent of many of the procedural safeguards that exist in the courts. With a broader toolkit, the PSO would possess the power to intervene more frequently, and in more depth, in areas of high policy to the inconvenience of existing political spheres of responsibility. Given the range of powers we are recommending, there is a reasonable concern that the office might duplicate other forms of administrative and regulatory control (Cabinet Office 2015: 16) or even become excessively entrepreneurial and pursue publicity and reputational gain in costly and ineffective interventions.

Such risks are real but the likelihood of them occurring should not be overstated, and the room for bad decisions and failed experiments in ombudsman practice to become embedded patterns of behaviour should be minimal provided suitable oversight is built into the new legislation. Further, the combined drivers of formal and informal scrutiny on the mindset of PSOs should not be underestimated. In recent years, some of the major transparency advances in the sector have come not from top-down oversight but internal endeavours to retain the trust of key stakeholders (see Chap. 8). To put it bluntly, it is in the interest of the PSO to demonstrate the legitimacy of its operations and to confront in advance concerns that it is inappropriately and ineffectively deploying its powers.

Notwithstanding the potential for the profession to control itself, the need for external scrutiny to promote trust in the institution is essential. As with the rest of the proposed new legislation, the design of the new accountability framework should be established in framework form to allow for adaptation to future events and learning. The accountability framework should be based upon three key areas: institutional design, reporting duties, and recognition of the rule of law.

Institutional Protection

The key formal oversight arrangements for the new PSO should be set up in legislation; these will include reference to the PSO's relationships with Parliament, the courts, audit, the government, and other watchdogs such as the Information Commissioner. Much of this set of relationships can be modelled on best practice as, for instance, set out in the *Vienna Principles on the Ombudsman* (Council of Europe 2019). However, Chap. 9 by Brian Thompson details two particular concerns that the new legislation should address: the relationship between Parliament and the new PSO, and the need to plan for ongoing, as opposed to ad hoc, scrutiny.

There are three dimensions to the ombudsman/Parliament relationship that could, and ideally should, be addressed separately in legislation as they are foundational to the office's effective operation: sponsorship, scrutiny, and support. Given this multi-dimensional relationship, we support the proposal implicit in the draft Bill to separate out some of the Parliamentary oversight duties between at least two distinct select committees. The introduction of the new PSO could be a symbolic moment for Parliament, whereby it takes enhanced ownership of the oversight and use of Parliamentary watchdogs such as the PSO. This solution would more clearly detail and embed the ombudsman/Parliament relationship than in the original 1967 Act, by clarifying the degree to which a committee is responsible for the appointment and funding (i.e. 'sponsorship') of the PSO. This solution would enable other select committees to focus on the 'scrutiny' and 'support' of the office. Inevitably, this latter set of functions would have to be confirmed in the Standing Orders of Parliament, but we would envisage this being the continued listed responsibility of the Public Administration and Constitutional Affairs Committee. Further support though should be encouraged from other select committees, depending on the area of government that the office is reporting on. In the long-term, there may be potential for a practice of joint-committee hearings and inquiries into the PSO's work given the breadth of core government responsibilities the office will oversee, such as central government, local government, and health.

On the need for ongoing scrutiny, experience of oversight of PSOs in the UK and elsewhere has demonstrated that such scrutiny is vital and can be extremely effective, but it also tends to be intermittent and occasionally of low quality. This may in part explain why the draft Bill put in place an innovative (at least for the ombudsman sector) solution: a corporate governance arrangement. By this arrangement, a statutory board would be established with the membership of the board appointed by Parliament. The responsibility of the board would be to scrutinise the work of the new PSO and account to Parliament for this function.

In outline, this is a powerful proposal which we support in the context of the PSO. The office will almost certainly become one of the largest in Europe and possess a very wide jurisdictional remit. Given past experience and the scale of work conducted by the UK Parliament, we are sceptical of Parliament's capacity to maintain a sufficiently high level of oversight of the PSO to satisfy demands for accountability of the office. In much of the public sector, this residual need for an added scrutiny capacity has been delivered through the introduction of a corporate governance arrangement (Cabinet Office 2017). However, the proposal raises a series of challenging questions for the Parliamentary/ombudsman relationship which will need to be addressed. Most importantly, the double layer of formal scrutiny of the PSO's work must not operate to neuter the office holder's ultimate responsibility for decision-making, particularly in terms of the outcome of individual investigations. Thus the role of the new board needs to be restricted to asking difficult questions of the office and where necessary reporting on inadequate performance to Parliament. This in turn raises another challenge, avoiding the PSO and the new board becoming rival sources of power which blur rather than clarify lines of responsibility (see Chap. 9 for further discussion of this issue).

We recommend one final institutional solution be incorporated into any new PSO legislation. There should be a requirement for the scheme to operate a quality assurance board made up of a cross-section of interested parties in the issues raised in the body's jurisdiction, for example representatives of users of services, providers, and regulators. Its role would be twofold: first, to provide increased assurance that fair and correct decisions are being made and second, to integrate a forum in which the standards being applied within the office are being challenged and tested from external perspectives (see Chap. 8).

The Rule of Law and the Courts

At present, legislation on PSOs is silent on the role of the courts in reviewing legal claims brought against the office. It is not recommended here that this position should change, as the inherent jurisdiction of the court to review a PSO does not require legislative support. This jurisdiction is a rarely deployed process (Kirkham and O'Loughlin forthcoming) and should be seen as an important additional backstop safeguard against error, as well as a potential identifier of weaknesses in the legislative arrangements.

In two respects though, the role of the courts should be clarified. First, as already argued, the PSO should be given power to refer legal questions to the court. Second, the current legal status of ombudsman reports, which is subtly different depending on the office concerned, should be confirmed in statute and streamlined. In statute, PSO decisions should be given authoritative force on matters of fact and findings (e.g. see *R v Commissioner for Local Administration ex p Eastleigh BC* [1988] QB 855; Law Commission 2011: paras. 5.115–133). This solution would bolster the status of PSO decisions, whilst retaining the existing legal position that public authorities can choose to decline to implement the recommendations of an ombudsman (*R (Nestwood Homes Developments Ltd) v South Holland District Council* [2014] EWHC 863 (Admin)), albeit under a requirement to provide good reasons for such a decision beyond merely cost or disagreement.

Table 2.2 Summary of principles for reform

Principle	*Core rationale*	*Examples of specific measures*
The PSO should have a bolder role within the administrative justice system.	The current emphasis on individual complaint-handling misrepresents both the PSO's current role and the true potential of the office in the administrative justice system. A bolder role is required that seeks to realise good administration in government and help bridge the gap between citizens and the state.	Statutory provisions should make clear the various roles the PSO is expected to play. Filtering powers should be made explicit in statute to allow the PSO to control demand for its services and adjust its priorities appropriately.
There should be a presumption in favour of the PSO having jurisdiction over all English public services, while respecting the UK's devolution settlement.	An integrated PSO provides the opportunity to raise the public profile of the office, reduce confusion for citizens, and join up investigation of public services. While the creation of an integrated English PSO is justified for the reasons above, a separate office is required to deal with UK-wide matters if the devolution settlement is to be respected.	A statutory duty should be imposed on government to give reasons should it decide that a stand-alone ombudsman is required in a particular jurisdiction. Separate legislation and visibly separate PSOs are required to deal with English public services and UK-wide public services.
The PSO should possess a broad toolkit of powers.	The realisation of a more ambitious and suitable role for the PSO requires a range of new powers for the office. Powers should be framed in broad ways that allow maximum flexibility for the PSO to develop practice over time and maintain relevance in changing circumstances.	The PSO should be empowered to conduct public interest investigations in the absence of a complaint being received. The PSO should be given 'Complaint Standards Authority' powers to oversee public service complaint-handling.

(*continued*)

Table 2.2 (continued)

Principle	*Core rationale*	*Examples of specific measures*
The PSO should be subject to a duty to report on engagement with citizens and delivery of administrative justice.	Citizens at large (not only those who complain) should be at the heart of the PSO's work and must be engaged in ways that allow for dialogue and co-production. Reflecting the PSO's proposed broader role, the PSO should be under a duty not only to report on its own performance but to report on the functioning of the administrative justice system as a whole and the degree to which good administration is being realised. Providing reporting duties, rather than burdensome legislative requirements, will help flexibility in the delivery of the PSO's service with appropriate opportunities for stakeholders to hold the PSO to account.	A range of duties to report activities should be included in statute.
The PSO should be subject to a range of accountability routes	The current oversight arrangements for PSOs are outdated and, if a larger, integrated, more powerful PSO is created these arrangements will become even more inadequate. To recognise the complexity of overseeing an independent administrative justice institution such as the PSO, multiple lines of accountability are required which respect to the office's independence while providing clear public evidence of effectiveness.	A corporate board, appointed by Parliament, should be set up to oversee the work of the PSO. Parliamentary committees should maintain a key, bifurcated role, in holding the PSO to account and supporting its work in bringing about good administration in the government. A quality assurance board, composed of stakeholders, should be set up to sample and review PSO decisions to give public assurance with regard to their quality.

Conclusion

We do not underestimate the practical challenges to introducing new legislation or the potential for various stakeholders to resist reform. New PSO legislation would likely be led by the Cabinet Office, which in the current political environment has an unprecedented workload. This chapter has suggested a principled basis for the conduct of legislative reform and a framework which policymakers can use to shape specific proposals. It may be that the model we have proposed is too ambitious but, at the very least, we hope that the approach we have suggested in this chapter helps to ensure that—whatever approach is finally adopted by legislators—full consideration is given to what roles the PSO should fulfil, the powers it needs, and the best way to making sure the accountable use of those powers. Table 2.2 below provides a summary of the principles we have outlined in the chapter, the key rationale for the proposals, and some examples of specific measures proposed in relation to each principle.

In conclusion, this chapter and this collection seek to draw together the extensive knowledge that already exists on the options available for legislative reform and demonstrate that a strong framework already exists to support the drafting of new legislation. For any new government, the creation of a PSO along the model we have proposed should be seen as a relatively low cost measure which would signal a powerful commitment to realising good administration and enhancing the relationship between citizens and the state.

References

Buck, T., Kirkham, R., & Thompson, B. (2011). *The Ombudsman Enterprise and Administrative Justice*. Farnham: Ashgate.

Cabinet Office. (2000). *Review of the Public Sector Ombudsmen in England*. London: Cabinet Office.

Cabinet Office. (2015). *A Public Service Ombudsman Government Response to Consultation*. Retrieved November 7, 2019, from https://assets.publishing.service.gov.uk/government/uploads/system/uploads/attachment_data/file/486797/PSO_-_Consultation_Response_-_Final.pdf.

Cabinet Office. (2016). *Draft Public Service Ombudsman Bill*. Cm. 9374.

Cabinet Office. (2017). *Corporate Governance in Central Government Departments*. Retrieved November 7, 2019, from https://assets.publishing.service.gov.uk/government/uploads/system/uploads/attachment_data/file/609903/PU2077_code_of_practice_2017.pdf.

Council of Europe. (2019). European Commission for Democracy Through Law (Venice Commission), *Principles on the Protection and Promotion of the Ombudsman Institution* (CDL-AD(2019)005).

Department of Health. (2017). *Draft Health Service Safety Investigations Bill*. Cm. 9497.

Drewry, G., & Harlow, C. (1990). A 'Cutting Edge'? The Parliamentary Commissioner and MPs. *Modern Law Review, 53*, 745.

Education Committee. (2019). *Special Education Needs and Disabilities*. HC 20.

Elliott, M. (2006). Asymmetric Devolution and Ombudsman Reform in England. *Public Law*, 84–105.

Gordon, R. (2014). *Better to Serve the Public: Proposals to Restructure, Reform, Renew and Reinvigorate Public Services Ombudsmen*. London: Cabinet Office.

Harlow, C. (2018). Ombudsmen: 'Hunting Lions' or 'Swatting Flies'. In M. Hertogh & R. Kirkham (Eds.), *Research Handbook on The Ombudsman*. Cheltenham: Edward Elgar.

Harlow, C., & Rawlings, R. (2009). *Law and Administration* (3rd ed.) Cambridge: CUP.

Heede, K. (2003). *European Ombudsman: Redress and Control at Union Level*. London: Kluwer Law International.

Home Affairs Committee. (2018). *The Windrush Generation*. (2017–19) HC 990.

Hubeau, B. (2018). The Profile of Complainants: How to Overcome the Matthew Effect? In M. Hertogh & R. Kirkham (Eds.), *Research Handbook on The Ombudsman*. Cheltenham: Edward Elgar.

Jersey Law Commission. (2018). *Designing a Public Services Ombudsman for Jersey*. Retrieved November 7, 2019, from https://jerseylawcommission.files.wordpress.com/2018/11/jsylawcom_designingombudsman_final.pdf.

Kirkham, R., & O'Loughlin, E. (forthcoming). Judicial Review and Ombuds: A Systematic Analysis. *Public Law*.

Law Commission. (2011). (Law Com No 329) *Public Services Ombudsmen*. HC 1136.

Ombudsman Association. (2019). *Criteria for the Recognition of Ombudsman Offices*. Retrieved October 31, 2019, from http://www.ombudsmanassociation.org/docs/OA-TermsandRulesJuly2019.pdf.

Tomlinson, J. (2019). Quick and Uneasy Justice: An Administrative Justice Analysis of the EU Settlement Scheme. Retrieved December 2, 2019, from https://ukaji.org/2019/07/16/quick-and-uneasy-justice-an-administrative-justice-analysis-of-the-eu-settlement-scheme/.

Work and Pensions Committee. (2018). *Universal Credit: Support for Disabled People*. (2017–19) HC 1770.

CHAPTER 3

The Public Services Ombud and the Claims of Democracy

Nick O'Brien

Abstract This chapter advances a theoretical basis for the development of a public ombud institution that is progressive and democratic. In so doing, it seeks to answer the question of what sort of public ombud we want and need. It offers a critical account of the apparent consensus on 'modern ombudsman practice', characterised by the prioritisation of the individual user, system and dispute resolution. It associates 'modern ombudsman practice' of this sort with a jurisprudential mentality, with the values of the 'new public management' and with the ideal of the quasi-judicial ombud and its priorities of negative individual rights, boundaries and adjudication. As an alternative, it proposes the democratic ombud founded upon the 'demosprudential' values of community, human rights principle and deliberative practice. It concludes that the demosprudential path is the necessary means of attaining 'the People's Ombud' and an ombud that is true to its democratic roots. This will require the acquisition by the ombud of different powers, as well as a willingness and capacity to use them.

Keywords Democracy • Community • Positive rights • Deliberation • Demosprudence

---

N. O'Brien (✉)
University of Liverpool, Liverpool, UK

R. Kirkham, C. Gill (eds.), *A Manifesto for Ombudsman Reform*,
https://doi.org/10.1007/978-3-030-40612-7_3

Introduction

This chapter is concerned with a general question: what sort of public services ombud (PSO) do we want in the UK (and more particularly in England, where reform has largely failed to keep pace with that in Northern Ireland, Scotland and Wales). Although the geographical focus is to that extent specific, the discussion involves issues that are relevant to PSOs elsewhere, as they too grapple with the legacies of legalism, managerialism and the subordination of egalitarian principles to libertarian forms of democracy. In answering that general question, the chapter reasserts the need for PSOs that are true to their democratic origins and that conform to the egalitarian and participatory claims of democracy upon it, both in the practices they adopt and in the values they promote. The aim is to advance a theoretical foundation for attaining that objective, not only in the interests of principle but with an eye to extracting maximum public value from the process of responding to individual grievance.

As such, the chapter seeks to challenge the apparent consensus, not just in the UK, on the preferred contours of 'modern ombudsman practice' (MOP) and its acceptance of a mentality that is shaped by legalistic concepts and 'new public management' (NPM) values. Such a mentality fatally constrains the extra-judicial potential of the ombud institution, condemning it to a role that is by contrast merely quasi-judicial. The democratic ombud by contrast is founded upon a theoretical platform that is demosprudential, not jurisprudential.

Demosprudence, as a potential approach to administrative justice, is contemporary in its articulation, but its practices, built on the ability of social movements or mobilised communities to make, interpret and change the law, are not new (Baxi 2016). Demosprudence is a vehicle for making the process of responding to citizen grievance more democratic and for situating law in broader cultural and political contexts. It is an idea in tension with those other forms of legal liberalism that favour a common law mentality that prioritises strict legal precedent, command and control enforcement, adversarialism, individualism and the strict separation of law from ethics, culture and politics. It celebrates in particular 'role-literate participants', who are focal points for articulating grievance. Such role-literate participants also act as 'bridging institutions' that enable successful connection across perceived boundaries and in that way 'ground and frame the discourse' (Allen 2004; Guinier 2009). The demosprudential literature cites as an example the dissenting judge, who, although in the minority, nevertheless draws on democratic perspectives (Ray 2011; Guinier and Torres 2014). Implicit in much that follows is the recognition that the ombud is also a role-literate participant, whose natural habitat is the demosprudential hinterland.[1] To achieve the democratic ombud recommended here entails firstly, designing the institution so that it has the mission and powers to delivery its underlying vision and, secondly, to embed different priorities in the operational management of ombud offices. Proposals for how this change of direction might be achieved are touched upon in the concluding section of this chapter.

Modern Ombudsman Practice: User, System, Resolution

The widespread recognition of MOP as a settled set of desirable characteristics may be supposed to have ended any further debate about the sort of ombud we want. The recent report in the UK of the Independent Peer Review of the Parliamentary and Health Service Ombudsman (PHSO) entitled the *Value for Money Study* (Tyndall et al. 2018), for example, takes MOP as its keynote and as its inevitable destination. MOP in this context, with at least implicit International Ombudsman Institute sanction, valorises effective and efficient service, stakeholder evaluation, robust management systems, quality assurance, easier public access, flexible and appropriate dispute resolution, professional accreditation and public accountability.

The dominant values of efficiency, effectiveness and economy, with an emphasis on the individual user, on system and on proportionate dispute resolution, are also those of NPM (Drewry 2009). MOP shares those NPM values and is therefore recognisable as the foundation for the 'managerial ombudsman' (Gill et al. 2019). This valorisation of user, system and resolution is especially receptive to a jurisprudential conception of ombud identity. MOP is an ally not only of the managerial ombudsman but of the quasi-judicial ombud also, with its focus on the delivery of individual resolution.

The way in which MOP, NPM and the quasi-judicial ombud have come to coalesce can be illustrated by reference to the arc of recent administrative justice reform in the UK. The PHSO *Value for Money* study, like the

[1] For further discussion of the general argument advanced here, see Doyle and O'Brien (2019).

draft *Public Services Ombudsman Bill* 2016 and the *Tribunals, Inquiries and Enforcement Act* 2007, effectively adopts the conceptual framework of the 2004 White Paper *Transforming Public Services: Complaints, Redress and Tribunals.* Three keywords define the White Paper's priorities. Firstly, there is 'user': the design proposals enshrined in the White Paper are unapologetically to be 'tested by a simple criterion: what is best for the users'. The answer to the question of what is best for the individual user is 'resolution': what the user wants above all is resolution of disputes, and preferably resolution that is quick, inexpensive, simple, rigorous, private and final, and, critically, proportionate to the dispute in question. Nipping problems in the bud through signposting and early resolution provided by a tailored dispute resolution service is the overriding ambition. The aim is to squeeze this service into a clearly demarcated 'system' and so achieve more systematic coherence. Following on from Leggatt's dismay in 2000 at the lack of any recognisable system in the way tribunals worked, the White Paper looked to the administrative justice landscape outside the tribunal sector and sought to extend the ambition of systematisation to all its component parts. These three keywords—'user', 'system' and 'resolution'—also informed the Administrative Justice and Tribunals Council's guardianship of administrative justice between 2007 and 2013. Its stated remit was, after all, to keep under review 'the administrative justice system as a whole with a view to making it accessible, fair and efficient' and to ensure that 'the relationships between the courts, tribunals and ombudsmen and alternative dispute resolution providers satisfactorily reflect the needs of users' (AJTC 2007).

The Quasi-judicial Ombud: Individual Negative Rights, Boundaries, Adjudication

The suggestion that MOP, and the programme of which it forms part, is permeated by NPM principles is consistent with the view that MOP sits comfortably in a quasi-judicial framework. Just as the ombud has increasingly shown consumerist and managerial tendencies since the 1980s, the implementation of the Leggatt proposals illustrates how the attitudes and behaviour of judges have also betrayed NPM influence during the same period (Resnick 1982). In shifting in a managerial direction, ombuds have merely shared an ethos that has shaped developments in the justice process more widely (Genn 2008). That consumerism and managerialism should have become the cosy bedfellows of a jurisprudential ethos can be gauged further from consideration of the underlying characteristics of a quasi-judicial mentality, especially as reflected in the chief tenets of conventional legal liberalism (Simon 2003, 2009).

Firstly, a jurisprudential mentality often has at its centre the individual bearer of civil and political rights, which are 'negative' in the sense that they prioritise liberty as freedom from interference, rather than as any more positive capability (Berlin 1969). The rights-bearer, according to this way of thinking, is a potential victim, whose interests are in conflict with those of public or private authorities who exercise power, or with other private individuals with whom they are in competition. This individual focus is reinforced by the romantic idea that everyone's 'case' is different and so must be quarantined from other such cases as far as possible (Simon 2003; Sugarman 1986).

Secondly, such a mentality also favours strong boundaries, to define separate functions, to separate law from politics and culture and to designate strongly defined remits, even where transgression of such boundaries appears necessary (Sugarman 1986). To that extent, the quasi-judicial mentality is systematic, in favour of strong bright lines of demarcation, and nervous of ambiguity.

Finally, a quasi-judicial mentality, once more reflecting its discomfort with ambiguity, values closure and prizes adjudication as its preferred method of social ordering (Fuller 1981). It is the ability to achieve resolution, to facilitate business as usual and allow the parties to move on that secures much of the perceived social value of legal intervention, especially in a market, or quasi-market, environment.

In these important respects, the ombud, as purveyor of MOP and NPM, and despite its extra-legal credentials, partakes of a strongly jurisprudential ethos. It is, for example, commonplace to assert that the core function of the ombud is the resolution of individual grievances, albeit tempered by a recognition of the desirability of 'learning from complaints'. Since the first discussions of the ombud in the UK in the 1950s, there has been a libertarian and individualist strain of thinking that has claimed the ombud as the friend of the 'little man (sic)' in the face of state intrusion and bureaucracy (Whyatt 1961; Utley 1961). That individualistic focus endures, with individual rights-bearers cast as the victims of callous or indifferent street-level bureaucrats and inefficient providers of public services.

Significant too are perennial concerns about the relationship between the ombud and the courts, the ombud and regulation, about 'mission-creep' more generally and about how far the ombud's remit overlaps with the power of judicial review, how it fits into the judicial system conceived as an integrated whole or indeed whether it constitutes a separate system of justice in its own right (Abraham 2008). Since the outset the Parliamentary Commissioner for Administration Act 1967 has enabled the ombud to reject a complaint on the grounds that there is an alternative legal remedy reasonably available elsewhere in the system. Although allowing a measure of discretion, such a provision has locked the ombud into a structure that is dominated by the courts and that casts its shadow over the ombud's practice (Harlow and Rawlings 2009). In 2011, the Law Commission engaged in detail with this provision and made recommendations for enabling more cross-reference between the courts and ombuds (Law Commission 2011). If such a recommendation had been implemented, it might easily have pushed the ombud further in a jurisprudential direction. Even in the absence of implementation, the very suggestion indicates the extent to which the ombud is encouraged to see itself as part of a system of regular boundaries in which the courts are the senior partner.

The aspiration towards adjudication and closure, although in theory defeated by the fact that the ombud is unable to enforce its recommendations, is nevertheless in practice encouraged by the positioning of the ombud as the final port of call. The drive towards proportionate dispute resolution, in particular, unavoidably positions the ombud as an essentially jurisprudential vehicle, albeit without the formal trappings of the courts. 'Proportionate' in this context is likely to equate to a cheaper and quicker means of doing what the courts do more expensively and slowly. The difference is essentially one of degree not of kind; the relationship of the ombud to the courts is that of a photographic negative to the photograph itself.

It has also been argued that, although less formally legalistic than, for example, its very legalistic German near-counterparts, the UK ombud is perceived by users in the shadow of the law, to the extent that a predetermined legal consciousness shapes expectations of the ombud (Creutzfeldt 2018). It is notable that 'ombud-watchers', and others, have criticised the ombud in effect for not being more judicial, for example, in its inability to achieve closure through enforceable decisions or to test evidence through a more adversarial process, or to make more objectively testable decisions by reference to fixed rules rather than vague principles.

In an era during which judicial review of its practice has remained a significant source of anxiety for ombuds, it is notable too that the higher courts have shown signs of exerting more direct control in the interests of legalism (Harlow and Rawlings 2009; Kirkham 2018).

In the UK, of particular importance for the jurisprudential turn in the ombud mentality was the creation of the Health Service Commissioner (HSC) function in 1973, with its service-deficit remit and eventually its clinical-judgement remit also. In this respect the practice of the HSC has been pushed inexorably towards an overtly quasi-judicial form, with the concerns of the Medical Defence Union, the Patients' Association and indeed the courts being framed in jurisprudential terms (e.g. about the applicability or otherwise of the strict legal test for clinical negligence). Since health cases now account for 80% of the PHSO's caseload, this tendency alone is especially revealing of the way in which a jurisprudential mentality has by necessity prevailed during the period since 1973 in particular. Moreover, the emphasis on individual decision-making derived from the legal concept of tort leaves little place for the analysis of systemic considerations. When conjoined with the 'legalistic' concept of maladministration that tortious approach leaves the ombud 'clinging to another narrow and incomplete understanding of what truly generates poor and unsafe care' (Donaldson 2018).

The embrace of dispute resolution, systematic integration and individual access betray therefore an underlying disposition that is consistent with, and has been shaped by, jurisprudential forms, by legal advisers both in the ombud's office and 'in office' (it is notable that during a formative period the individual Parliamentary and Health Service Commissioners were lawyers), and by the judge over the ombud's shoulder.

This jurisprudential construction of ombud identity is by now well entrenched. Even before 1973 it had been anticipated that a health service ombud would be in danger of becoming a clearing house for NHS complaints lodged by health service consumers (Crick 1965; Stein 1971); and by 1978, it was feared that the Parliamentary Ombudsman, in its search for a role, might 'degenerate' into a small claims court (Harlow 1978). Before long, a firmly quasi-judicial mentality had taken hold, in which the judiciary and the model of litigation as dispute resolution dominated. Judicial review, although never frequent, attracted disproportionate attention and cast a shadow over ombud practice. Any aspiration towards extra-legal informality or towards using the ombud to shape the state in a 'cult of bureaucratic humanity' (Shonfield 1965) was to that extent defeated in favour of a much more jurisprudential ombud, especially once the office passed between 1979 and 1990 into the hands of successive lawyers, Sir Cecil Clothier and Sir Anthony Barrowclough, who left an indelible mark on the institution (Gregory and Giddings 2002; Harlow 1978; Harlow and Rawlings 2009).

The Democratic Ombud: Community, Positive Human Rights Principle and Deliberative Decision-Making

The basis for the construction of an alternative to the quasi-judicial ombud can be found in demosprudence. Stefan Hurwitz, the influential first Danish Ombudsman, told the British public in 1959 about the democratic credentials of the ombud institution (Hurwitz 1960). Just as importantly, the ombud was to be seen in the light of its Scandinavian provenance as an agent of communitarian or public benefit rather than primarily a source of dispute resolution or individual redress. The fact that the Danish ombud had discretion to launch an investigation in the public interest, even in the absence of a specific complaint from an individual, was further evidence that individual dispute resolution did not, even from the outset, dominate his work (Holm 1995: 19–20; Busck 1995). Complaints were always capable of being seen not so much as a gift but as a distraction (Harlow and Rawlings 2009).

This Scandinavian democratic vision fitted well with post-war aspirations in Britain. The task of how to reform the often high-handed behaviour of officials to fit a new democratic ethos was urgent. The disregard, for example, of local-authority housing officers for their tenants was notorious (Williams 1961). There are still echoes of those sentiments in the wake of the Grenfell Tower fire and the investigation of its antecedents; in the depiction of the welfare benefits system in Ken Loach's film *I, Daniel Blake*; and in the empirical investigation of the benefits system itself against norms of dignity and respect (Adler 2018).

When, half a century after Hurwitz's call to arms, the Public Administration Select Committee reported on the PHSO in 2014, it called its report *Time for a People's Ombudsman*. The immediate spur to the report was the loss of confidence in NHS regulation entailed by the Francis Report on the Mid-Staffordshire NHS Foundation Trust and the encouragement from the EU Alternative Dispute Resolution Directive and On-line Dispute Resolution Regulations for ombuds to see themselves increasingly as mass dispute resolution mechanisms. At the same time, digital-era governance,

TripAdvisor consumerism and the erosion of publicly funded advice services challenged existing methods of working. A new era of direct popular participation seemed both possible and necessary in an age of unparalleled technological development.

PASC responded with a programme of simplification and rationalisation: a single point of entry for all public service complaints, a single PSO for England and a single Cabinet Office minister with responsibility for complaints and ombud policy. The title of the PASC Report on the Ombudsman also points towards the need for renewed democratic engagement. The idea of the People's Ombudsman, as opposed to that of Parliament's Ombudsman, suggests a shift of emphasis from a model of representative democracy towards something more participatory. That shift is especially signalled by the proposal to remove the MP filter and the need for complaints to be formalised in writing. A call for enhanced outreach work is also implicit in the recognised need for the Ombudsman to complete more investigations to ensure that disadvantaged and marginalised individuals and communities are encouraged to see themselves as part of the ombud's natural constituency and not as outsiders.

Consistent with the ambition to make the ombud institution more democratic or 'popular' is the proposed introduction of a power of 'own-initiative' investigation. Although such a power could be wielded in the interest of intensified NPM oversight, there is also democratic potential in the ability to investigate where there is well-founded suspicion, yet the circumstances of those most directly affected, for example, in prisons, care homes or psychiatric units, or otherwise marginalised, as in the recent treatment by the Home Office of the Windrush Generation, make it unlikely that an individual complaint will be brought. The undesirability in principle of reliance on individual grievance as a means of delivering substantive justice and meaningful reform more generally has, for example, recently been reinforced by the conclusions of a select committee inquiry into the operation of the Equality Act 2010. Noting the 'limitations of individual enforcement', the Women and Equalities Committee has identified once more the need for a 'fundamental shift' from 'individualised approaches' to something more 'proactive and preventative' that can scale up the existing duties so that they become more 'focused' and 'strategic' (Women and Equalities Committee 2019).

The measures proposed by PASC, cumulatively, presage in principle more participation and practical engagement in the decision-making process. The style of investigation undertaken by the ombud, already inquisitorial (at least in theory) rather than adversarial, and revisable to the extent that the investigation unfolds over time and through the reiterative contributions of the parties themselves, is well suited in principle to a deliberative style. Additionally, the ombud's investigatory style is based on the need to achieve a measure of consensus and to do so by facilitating active participation in what at its best amounts to a process of public reasoning on the issues raised by citizen grievance. PASC's proposals may to that extent be seen to reinforce a distinctive style of ombud social ordering that is neither formal, in the sense of being legally enforceable, nor entirely informal, in the sense of being the product of unfettered participant negotiation. When seen in that light, the proposals have the potential to be recognised as deliberative, democratic and incipiently demosprudential.

When it comes to the norms, or standards, rules and principles against which they evaluate the grievances referred to them, ombuds typically claim to make their decisions on the basis of what is fair and reasonable in the particular case. They are not rigorously bound by precedent, like common law courts. Their approach is more like a form of equity than common law adjudication. There is, however, an attendant, and not always welcome, element of vagueness. PASC suggests ways in which norms that are transparent and rooted in principle rather than rules might be promoted: firstly, by publicising decisions more widely (for instance, see Chap. 8) and, secondly, by taking on the role of complaints design authority, as in Scotland, and in a manner that goes well beyond PHSO's *Principles of Good Administration, Complaint Handling, and Redress* (for instance, see Chap. 6). Such measures might easily serve merely to promote NPM principles. However, in the context of PASC's call for the People's Ombudsman, a more integrated interpretation would be to suggest that their equally valid function should be to encourage deliberative decision-making in accordance with positive human rights principle, especially when they touch upon positive social rights entitlement in areas such as healthcare, social care, housing and education (O'Brien 2009; O'Brien and Thompson 2010).

It is possible therefore to interpret PASC's call for a People's Ombudsman as progressive and not merely as trite reinforcement of NPM values. At the heart of such an interpretation rests a democratic suite of preferences: for democratic participation, for community engagement with the practice of human rights principle and for deliberative decision-making. If such preferences are to be sustainable, they need to be rooted in a legal-theoretical framework that is not merely jurisprudential but instead demosprudential.

The literature of legal pragmatism and deliberative problem-solving provides a demosprudential theory that makes sense of the role of the people in law-making and implementation, and in the practice of social movements (Simon 2003, 2009; Klein 2007; Sabel and Simon 2004; Chayes 1976; Menkel-Meadow 2004–2005, 2006; Gutmann and Thompson 2004; Dorf and Sabel 1998; Berman and Feinblatt 2001; Hertogh 2001). In short, instead of prioritising individual victims, such approaches emphasise citizen empowerment and the common good, principles as norms rather than rules, deliberation instead of adversarialism and an iterative process instead of closure and final resolution.

The translation of these more deliberative and experimental approaches into problem-solving courts has encouraged the prospect of better outcomes for the parties to a dispute as well as more public benefit for broader communities, for example in the development of community courts as a model for domestic-violence courts and mental health courts in the US (Berman and Feinblatt 2001). In other contexts the courts themselves have effectively been re-structured, demosprudentially, to enable not just public interest litigation but a more democratically authentic process for addressing social rights disputes in a forum that is both deliberative and democratic (Fredman 2008). Elsewhere, the ombud itself has acted as a dynamic and demosprudential role-literate participant and focal-point for popular dissent (Pegram 2008, 2013; Peruzzotti 2012). Closer to home, for example in an equality and human rights context, a broadly demosprudential approach has been advocated by policy makers (Hepple et al. 2000) and pursued by practitioners as part of the 'new civil rights history' (O'Brien 2016). At its best, mediation, especially as informed by a rights-based approach, also discloses features that are democratic and consistent with a demosprudential foundation (Doyle 2019; Doyle and O'Brien 2019).

In the context of UK PSO reform, there are already elements of PHSO and Local Government and Social Care Ombudsman (LGSCO) practice that presage a demosprudential future, notwithstanding the constraints of an underlying quasi-judicial mentality. Some of those elements are acknowledged in *Value for Money*: the development of outreach work through initiatives such as Radio Ombudsman; the increased transparency of outcomes and of communication more generally; the purposeful publication of special thematic reports on issues such as mental health, sepsis and the treatment of eating disorders, and in the case of the LGSCO on special educational needs or refuse collection; the re-articulated aspiration to acquire own-initiative investigation powers, complaints design-authority powers and scope to develop flexible methods of response to grievance. In the recent PHSO past as well there is precedent for a demosprudential approach that has, for example, combined NGO activism with the invocation of human rights principle on behalf of a community of disadvantaged citizens (O'Brien 2011); and indeed examples of similar approaches can be traced back even further, for example, to the Channel Tunnel investigation during the 1990s (Harlow and Rawlings 2009), as well as forward to the contemporary and increasing advocacy by office-holders for own-initiative investigation powers.

Conclusion

The aim of this chapter has been to suggest that, desirable though legislative reform might be, ultimately a more popular and democratic future rests not only upon the ombud's acquisition of different powers but on the willingness and capacity to use those powers to develop different types of relationship with the legislature and the judiciary, and critically with the people. In that way the overarching relationship with the executive can be one that, in solidarity and integrity with the democratic origins of the ombud, serves to humanise the state bureaucracy and its encounters with citizens.

The problem of bureaucracy, with which the ombud is inextricably implicated, is fundamentally a 'problem in relationships' (Morris Jones 1949), in particular between citizen and state, and configured through the classical constitutional vehicles of legislature, judicature, executive and people. Whereas the quasi-judicial ombud is shaped by jurisprudential concepts and its relationship with the judiciary, the democratic ombud is shaped by demosprudential values and its overriding relationship with the demos, the people. Demosprudence is a theory of law that prioritises participatory relationships and the creation of 'bridges' between different interests. It is related to ideas such as public interest law, network governance, democratic experimentalism, legal pragmatism, therapeutic justice, deliberative democracy and problem-solving courts. It is a theory of law that invites the ombud to operate as a 'bridging' institution and thereby as an important component of a 'connected society', marked by a form of 'egalitarian participatory democracy' and by 'bridging ties' that enable successful interaction across boundaries. The connected society is a society in which a whole political community is engaged equally in the co-creation of a shared public life and of shared public institutions (Allen 2004).

The demosprudential ombud is quite simply 'the People's Ombudsman', identified in 2014 by PASC as the necessary destination of ombud reform, and conceived in this chapter as a key facilitator of that necessary practice of democratic co-creation. The 'art of bridging' and the practices of 'role-literate participant' offer the ombud the prospect of humanising those relationships between citizen and state; of reinforcing the bridging capacities, skills and knowledge of street-level bureaucrats and public authorities and of countering their pathological tendencies towards indifference, paternalism and rigid enforcement (Zacka 2017). Against those tendencies the ombud acknowledges also that the practices of bureaucracy extend beyond technical decision-making and the application of established rules. Instead, the ombud engages with a complex bureaucratic realm that necessarily prioritises certain values and interests over others, and that requires a high degree of responsiveness, not just efficiency, fairness and respect. Bureaucracy is in effect a 'crucible' in which abstract values acquire practical meaning. In such a context, the ombud emerges as an agent of public good rather than merely private benefit or redress, and moreover as a form of public good that is egalitarian and democratic (Nonet and Selznick 1978; Zacka 2017).

Demosprudence is more concerned with relationships than with powers or functions. Nevertheless, law reform can reinforce a change of emphasis. As explored in other chapters in this collection, a green light to own-initiative investigations, easier gathering and sharing of intelligence, and less constrained communication options would help overcome the limitations of reliance on individual complaints and enhance the public benefit to be derived from individual grievance. An acknowledged preference for principles over rules, for social rights principles over NPM values and for networks of accountability agencies over a mechanised system of justice would better reflect the realities of contemporary understandings of effective regulation, communication and institutional change. Recognition that in a complex environment closure is rarely achievable or even desirable would entail celebration of non-enforceable outcomes, deliberative and inclusive processes, and remedy, not just 'resolution', that is innovative and restorative. Demosprudence speaks powerfully to such aspirations and offers a framework in which the spirit of progressive reform can be captured. In so doing it offers an answer to the question of what sort of ombud we should want and of what relationships it should prioritise and nurture.

References

Abraham, A. (2008). The Ombudsman and "Paths to Justice": A Just Alternative or Just an Alternative? *Public Law*, p. 1.

Adler, M. (2018). *Cruel, Inhuman or Degrading Treatment: Benefit Sanctions in the UK*. London: Palgrave Pivot.

AJTC (2007). Tribunals, Courts and Enforcement Act 2007.

Allen, D. (2004). *Talking to Strangers: Anxieties of Citizenship Since*. Brown v. Board of Education. Chicago: University of Chicago Press.

Baxi, U. (2016). Law, Politics, and Constitutional Hegemony: The Supreme Court, Jurisprudence, and Demosprudence. In S. Choudhry, M. Khosla, & P. B. Mehta (Eds.), *The Oxford Handbook of the Indian Constitution*. Oxford: OUP.

Berlin, I. (1969). Two Concepts of Liberty. In I. Berlin (Ed.), *Four Essays on Liberty*. Oxford: OUP.

Berman, G., & Feinblatt, J. (2001). *Problem-Solving Courts: A Brief Primer*. New York: Center for Court Innovation.

Busck, L. (1995). The History and Development of the Institution of Ombudsman. In H. Gammeltoft-Hansen (Ed.), *The Danish Ombudsman*. Copenhagen: The Danish Ombudsman.

Chayes, A. (1976). The Role of the Judge in Public Law Litigation. *Harvard Law Review, 89*, 1281.

Creutzfeldt, N. (2018). *Ombudsmen and ADR: A Comparative Study of Informal Justice in Europe*. Geneva: Palgrave Macmillan.

Crick, B. (1965). The Prospects for Parliamentary Reform. *Political Quarterly, 36*, 333.

Donaldson, L. (2018). *Report of the Independent Adviser to the Clinical Advice Review Commissioned by the Parliamentary and Healthcare Ombudsman*. London: PHSO.

Dorf, M. C., & Sabel, C. F. (1998). A Constitution of Democratic Experimentalism. *Columbia Law Review, 98*, 267.

Doyle, M. (2019). *A Place at the Table: A Report on Young People's Participation in Resolving Disputes About Special Educational Needs and Disabilities*. Colchester: UKAJI.

Doyle, M., & O'Brien, N. (2019). *Reimagining Administrative Justice: Human Rights in Small Places*. London: Palgrave Macmillan.

Drewry, G. (2009). The Judicialisation of "Administrative" Tribunals in the UK: From Hewart to Leggatt. *Transylvanian Review of Administrative Sciences, 28*, 45.

Fredman, S. (2008). *Human Rights Transformed: Positive Rights and Positive Duties*. Oxford: OUP.

Fuller, L. (1981). The Forms and Limits of Adjudication. In K. L. Winston (Ed.), *The Principles of Social Order*. Durham, NC: Duke University Press.

Genn, H. (2008). *Judging Civil Justice. Hamlyn Lectures.* Cambridge: Cambridge University Press.

Gill, C., Mullen, T., & Vivian, N. (2020). The Managerial Ombuds. *Modern Law Review*. Forthcoming.

Gregory, R., & Giddings, P. (2002). *The Ombudsman, the Citizen and Parliament: A History of the Office of the Parliamentary Commissioner for Administration and Health Service Commissioners.* London: Politico's Publishing.

Guinier, L. (2009). Courting the People: Demosprudence and the Law/Politics Divide. *Boston University Law Review, 89*, 539.

Guinier, L., & Torres, G. (2014). Changing the Wind: Notes Towards a Demosprudence of Law and Social Movements. *Yale Law Journal, 123*, 2742.

Gutmann, A., & Thompson, D. (2004). *Why Deliberative Democracy?* Princeton: Princeton University Press.

Harlow, C. (1978). Ombudsmen in Search of a Role. *Modern Law Review, 41*, 446.

Harlow, C., & Rawlings, R. (2009). *Law and Administration* (3rd ed.). Cambridge: CUP.

Hepple, B., Coussey, M., & Choudhury, T. (2000). *Equality: A New Framework: Report of the Independent Review of the Enforcement of UK Anti-discrimination Legislation.* Oxford: Hart.

Hertogh, M. (2001). Coercion, Co-operation and Control: Understanding the Policy Impact of Administrative Courts and the Ombudsman in the Netherlands. *Law and Policy, 23*, 47.

Holm, N. E. (1995). The Ombudsman – A Gift from Scandinavia to the World. In H. Gammeltoft-Hansen (Ed.), *The Danish Ombudsman.* Copenhagen: The Danish Ombudsman.

Hurwitz, S. (1960, May 12). Interview with H.W.R. Wade and J.A.G.Griffiths. *The Listener.*

Kirkham, R. (2018). Safeguarding Procedural Fairness or Imposing Excessive Legalism? Retrieved November 13, 2019, from https://ukaji.org/2018/03/05/safeguarding-procedural-fairness-or-imposing-excessive-legalism/.

Klein, A. (2007–2008). Judging as Nudging: New Governance Approaches for the Enforcement of Constitutional Social and Economic Rights. *Columbia Human Rights Law Review, 39*, 351.

Law Commission. (2011). *Public Services Ombudsmen.* Report no 329. London: Law Commission.

Menkel-Meadow, C. (2004–2005). The Lawyer's Role(s) in Deliberative Democracy. *Nevada Law Journal, 5*, 347.

Menkel-Meadow, C. (2006). Deliberative Democracy and Dispute Resolution: Two Theories and Practices of Participation in the Polity. *Dispute Resolution Magazine*, p. 18.

Morris Jones, W. H. (1949). *Socialism and Bureaucracy.* London: Fabian Society.

Nonet, P., & Selznick, P. (1978). *Toward Responsive Law: Law and Society in Transition*. New York: Harper Torch.
O'Brien, N. (2009). Ombudsmen and Social Rights Adjudication. *Public Law*, p. 466.
O'Brien, N. (2011). Law and "The Good Life": Learning Disability, Equality and Healthcare in the UK. *The Equal Rights Review, 6*, 83.
O'Brien, N. (2016). Disability Discrimination Law in the United Kingdom and the New Civil Rights History: The Contribution of Caroline Gooding. *Journal of Law and Society, 43*, 444.
O'Brien, N., & Thompson, B. (2010). Human Rights and Accountability in the UK: Deliberative Democracy and the Role of the Ombudsman. *European Human Rights Law Review, 5*, 504.
Pegram, T. (2008). Accountability in Hostile Times: The Case of the Peruvian Human Rights Ombudsman 1996–2001. *Journal of Latin American Studies, 40*, 51.
Pegram, T. (2013). The Bolivian Human Rights Ombudsman and Economic, Social and Cultural Rights. In E. Brems, G. de Beco, & W. Vandenhole (Eds.), *National Human Rights Institutions, and Economic, Social and Cultural Rights*. Intersentia: Antwerp.
Peruzzotti, E. (2012). The Societalization of Horizontal Accountability: Rights Advocacy and the Defensor del Pueblo de la Nacion in Argentina. In R. Goodman & T. Pegram (Eds.), *Human Rights, State Compliance, and Social Change*. Cambridge: CUP.
Ray, B. (2011). Demosprudence in Comparative Perspective. *Stanford Journal of International Law, 47*, 111.
Resnick, J. (1982). Managerial Judges. *Harvard Law Review, 96*, 924.
Sabel, C. F., & Simon, W. H. (2004). Destabilization Rights: How Public Law Litigation Succeeds. *Harvard Law Review, 117*, 1016.
Shonfield, A. (1965). Modern Capitalism: the changing balance of public and private power (London, OUP: 1965).
Simon, W. H. (2003). *Solving Problems v Claiming Rights: The Pragmatist Challenge to Legal Liberalism*. Columbia Law School Public Law and Legal Theory Working Paper Group 03-58.
Simon, W. H. (2009). *The Warren Court, Legalism and Democracy: Sketch for a Critique in a Style Learned from Morton Horwitz*. Columbia Law School Public Law and Legal Theory Working Group Paper 09-196.
Stein, R. (1971). Accountability in the NHS. *Political Quarterly, 42*, 363.
Sugarman, D. (1986). Legal Theory, the Common Law Mind and the Making of the Textbook Tradition. In W. Twining (Ed.), *Legal Theory and Common Law*. Oxford: Blackwell.
Tyndall, P., Mitchell C., & Gill, C. (2018) *Value for Money Study: Report of the Independent Peer Review of the Parliamentary and Health Service Ombudsman*. Retrieved November 8, 2019, from https://www.ombudsman.org.uk/sites/default/files/Value_for_Money_report_final.pdf.

Utley, T. E. (1961). *Occasion for Ombudsman*. London: Christopher Johnson.
Whyatt, S. J. (1961). *The Citizen and the Administration: The Redress of Grievances*. London: Stevens & Sons.
Williams, R. (1961). *The Long Revolution*. London: Chatto and Windus.
Women and Equalities Committee. (2019). Enforcing the Equality Act: The Law and the Role of the Equalities and Human Rights Commission. HC 1470. Tenth Report of Session 2017–19.
Zacka, B. (2017). *When the State Meets the Street: Public Service and Moral Agency*. Cambridge, MA: Harvard University Press.

CHAPTER 4

The Ombud's Jurisdiction: Integration, Specialism, and Territorial Scope

Carolyn Hirst and Chris Gill

Abstract This chapter considers the scope of the ombud's jurisdiction. On the one hand, it argues for an integrated approach to English public services; on the other, it argues for reverting back to a standalone Parliamentary Ombud for UK-wide public services. In reaching this conclusion, the chapter sets out seven jurisdiction-based principles for reform. When assessed against these principles, the current draft Public Services Ombudsman Bill has a number of weaknesses: it fails to recognise the increasing blurring between public and private service provision; it does not recognise the need for the ombud's jurisdiction to reflect the devolution settlement; it takes an unprincipled approach to integration; and it fails to consider how sensitivity to different service user needs can be maintained within an integrated public service ombud.

C. Hirst
Queen Margaret University, Musselburgh, UK
e-mail: chirst@qmu.ac.uk

C. Gill (✉)
University of Glasgow, Glasgow, UK
e-mail: Chris.Gill@glasgow.ac.uk

R. Kirkham, C. Gill (eds.), *A Manifesto for Ombudsman Reform*,
https://doi.org/10.1007/978-3-030-40612-7_4

Keyword Ombud's jurisdiction • Ombuds integration • Ombuds specialisation • Devolution

Introduction

This chapter is about the ombud's jurisdiction and, particularly, the degree to which a specialist or integrated jurisdiction is to be preferred and whether distinct ombuds are required to cover England-only, England and Wales-only, and UK-wide central government departments and agencies. The UK's redress landscape is complex and fragmented and is the result of unprincipled and ad hoc development over time (Bondy and Le Sueur 2012). This phenomenon is reflected in the ombuds sector here (Kirkham 2019) and also in other jurisdictions, such as Australia (Stuhmcke 2016).

The current ombuds landscape for UK-wide, England, Wales, and Scotland-only, England and Wales-only, and England-only public services is shown in Table 4.1 over the page[1] and is complicated by its historical evolution and the process of devolution (Elliott 2006). It has been regularly suggested over the years that the basic argument for reversing history and harmonising ombuds is that the multiple schemes in England do not always map onto the delivery of twenty-first-century public services in a comprehensible, efficient, or effective manner (Kirkham and Martin 2014; Cabinet Office 2015a). Meanwhile in the UK's devolved jurisdictions, in Scotland, Wales, and Northern Ireland, devolution has provided the opportunity to create fully integrated, 'one-stop-shop', public services ombuds (PSOs), demonstrating what can be achieved.

In considering these issues, the chapter will firstly provide an overview of recent policy debates in relation to the optimal scope for the ombud's jurisdiction before raising a series of design questions that legislators will have to consider when finalising the new scheme. It argues that resolving jurisdiction questions is a fundamental challenge that will need to be addressed and suggests structuring that challenge through the consideration of four key factors: ombud type (whether public, private, or public interest), territorial scope (England, England and Wales, or UK), remit (specialist or integrated), and size. In doing so, the chapter makes a series of recommendations, which include a few provocative suggestions for reform. For instance, it argues that thought should be given to the inte-

[1] The table excludes ombuds who oversee privatised industries which continue to be of significant public interest, for example, The Rail Ombudsman, Ombudsman Services: Energy.

Table 4.1 Full territorial scope of public services ombuds with an English remit

Ombuds	*Public services covered*	*Territorial scope*
Parliamentary Ombudsman	UK central government department, agencies, Non Departmental Public Bodies (NDPBs), Quangos, and so on.	UK; England, Wales, and Scotland; England and Wales; England[a]
Health Services Ombudsman[b]	National health service	England
Local Government and Social Care Ombudsman	Local government and social care (including private social care providers)	England
Housing Ombudsman	Local government housing and registered social landlords	England
Office of the Independent Adjudicator for Higher Education	Higher education (including private universities)	England and Wales
Prisons and Probation Ombudsman	Prisons	England and Wales
Independent Office for Police Conduct	Police	England and Wales
Service Complaints Ombudsman for the Armed Forces	Armed forces	UK-wide

[a]The jurisdiction of the Parliamentary Ombudsman includes bodies with different territorial remits.
[b]Despite being separate statutory offices, in practice the offices Parliamentary Ombudsman and Health Services Ombudsman are held by the same person and the organisation is known publicly as the Parliamentary and Health Services Ombudsman

gration of Higher Education and Housing jurisdictions into the new scheme. At the same time, it suggests that matters of central government currently overseen by the Parliamentary Ombudsman should be separated out of the scheme in order to honour the devolution settlement. Finally, the chapter argues that one way to structure the new scheme would be by way of a college arrangement, whereby listed individual jurisdictions are required by statute to be overseen by a nominated post under the overall supervision of a Chief Ombudsman.

Recent Policy Debates

Discussions relating to integrating ombuds in England have taken place for over 20 years. There has been a prevailing view that integration is 'a good thing'. For example, current Cabinet Office (2010) guidance to UK government departments when considering setting up a new ombud scheme is that the role and remit of existing ombud schemes should be considered before deciding whether a new scheme is necessary. The development of unified PSOs in the devolved nations has also helped to give momentum to the idea that integration should be the default position in relation to setting the jurisdiction of ombuds. Recently, pressure for a unified PSO in the English context was intensified by two inquiries and associated reports by the Public Administration Select Committee of the UK Parliament. *More complaints please!* in 2014 set out the need for health and social care to work together and provide systemic solutions to the perceived systemic defects (PASC 2014a). Also in 2014, *Time for a People's Ombudsman Service* had the central finding that the Parliamentary and Health Ombudsman (PHSO) was 'stuck in time' and urgently in need of modernisation (PASC 2014b).

The 2014 Gordon Review (2014) recommended that the new ombud should at least encompass the Parliamentary and Health Services Ombudsman (PHSO) and the Local Government Ombudsman and Social Care Ombudsman (LGSCO), with a question mark over the inclusion of the Housing Ombudsman Service (HOS). Responses to the government consultation (Cabinet Office 2015a) on proposed draft legislation broadly supported a single service encompassing existing PHSO and LGSCO jurisdictions, with a framework allowing others to join over time (Cabinet Office 2015b). However, the draft *Public Service Ombudsman Bill* (draft Bill) did not appear in the Queen's Speech and has been widely criticised as insufficiently ambitious with ongoing pressure for reform (Kirkham 2019).

Meanwhile, developments in relation to private sector ombuds have also suggested some moves towards integration, albeit complicated by a continued interest from the UK government in encouraging competition between redress providers (Gill et al. 2017). In 2002, eight separate bodies were merged to form the UK Financial Ombudsman Service (FOS), a single 'one-stop-shop' ombuds, in order 'to reduce confusion and possible duplication, especially so far as consumers are concerned, while responding to the blurring of traditional distinctions between the industry sectors' (Financial Ombudsman Service 2000). Other UK private sector ombuds have widened sectoral jurisdictions through incremental additions.[2] Some private sector ombuds have an 'umbrella' set up that allows them to run

[2] Such as the former Furniture Ombudsman (now the Dispute Resolution Ombudsman) including traders in the retail and home improvement industries.

distinct ombudsman schemes under the same 'brand' (e.g. Ombudsman Services which includes, *inter alia*, the energy ombudsman and the communications ombudsman). There have also been some moves to simplify provision in sectors where several ombuds operate, with Ombudsman Services withdrawing from the property sector in August 2018, saying this decision was taken due to 'the disjointed and confusing landscape which currently exists' (Ombudsman Services 2018: 8).

To Integrate or Not to Integrate? Four Factors to Consider

Questions around integration have therefore been an important theme in recent policy, but the underlying value of integration has not always been explicitly set out and there has been little focused attention on its advantages and disadvantages. Seneviratne (2006) puts forward arguments for integration relating to:

- changes in delivery of public services;
- jurisdictional gaps and overlaps;
- efficiencies;
- customer focus; *and*
- opportunities for a higher profile service.

Other arguments in favour of integration are the resulting economies of scale and enhancing expertise within the ombud office itself (Kirkham 2019), and the removal of limits on the ability to secure systemic change related to the narrowness of current jurisdiction, with integration allowing for sharing of learning across jurisdictions (Tyndall et al. 2018). The relatively few arguments against integration are mainly based around retaining sector-specific expertise so as to maintain respect and authority amongst key stakeholders (such as the confidence that the organisation has expert insight of a sector) and the benefits of having recognisable and accessible figureheads within the different sectors (House of Commons Library 2016). The rest of this chapter aims to bring more clarity to debates around integration by examining four factors that should be considered when setting the scope of an ombud's jurisdiction: type, territorial scope, remit, and size. For each factor, key issues that policymakers need to consider are drawn out and principles are set out in order to inform the next phase of legislative reform.

Type—Public, Private, or Public Interest?

Consideration is required of whether a strict distinction between public and private ombuds (and public and private services generally) should be maintained in future. The current opportunity for legislative reform provides a chance to consider whether the public-private divide that characterises the current UK landscape remains relevant. The term 'type' here, therefore, relates to whether an ombuds has a public sector (concerned with the administration of government and the delivery of public services) or private sector (concerned with those operating in the goods and service economy) focus. A wide range of public services are now delivered by private companies, charities, and not-for-profit agencies under contracts with public authorities, such as the running of immigration removal centre and the provision of social care. Many formerly public services have also been privatised, such as rail and utilities, despite the fact that such services provide public goods. As a result, the boundaries between private and public provisions are increasingly unclear.

The Council of Europe's Venice Principles (2019) state that 'The institutional competence of the Ombudsman shall cover public administration at all levels. The mandate of the Ombudsman shall cover all general interest and public services provided to the public, whether delivered by the State, by the municipalities, by State bodies or by private entities'. Also, International Ombudsman Institute (2017) guidance considers that new ombud schemes should provide full coverage of all public services, whether delivered by the State, by municipalities or State bodies, on behalf of the State or by independent bodies or companies. These international guidelines support the view that the reformed ombud's jurisdiction should include both those who receive public funding and those who carry out functions of a public nature or where there is a significant public interest in the service being delivered (irrespective of their funding source).

To some extent this is taking place already. The jurisdiction of the LGSCO was extended in October 2010 to include adult social care not funded by the local authority (Health Act 2009: s.35). There is also precedent for extending the health remit in the UK as the Public Services Ombudsman (Wales) Act 2019 will allow the PSOW to investigate 'other health-related services', if without doing so, the PSOW is unable to completely investigate the relevant action by the public service health provider. In both of these areas, the service subject to review by the ombud is essentially the same, as is the level of public interest involved, irrespective of the funding source.

In other countries, ombuds span the public/private divide more explicitly. For example, Stuhmcke (2012) has described the growth in 'classical' ombud's jurisdiction to cover previously private sector services. In Australia, the Tasmanian Ombudsman is the State's Parliamentary Ombudsman, the Health Complaints Commissioner (dealing with complaints in both public and private sectors) and also the Energy Ombudsman. However, the potential to integrate public and private ombuds has featured very little in current debates within the UK. The recent Jersey Law Commission report (2018) on the creation of a PSO for Jersey did consider whether a new PSO scheme could work with the existing Channel Islands Financial Ombudsman and concluded that people seeking to use the two organisations (consumers of financial services and citizens aggrieved by government) were likely to have different needs. While the potential for integrating a financial ombuds with a public ombuds may be limited, there might be other areas where mixed public and private jurisdictions might be more appropriate (rail and energy being potential examples).

Housing provides a particularly good example of the way that boundaries between public and private service provision are becoming eroded. Council housing is considered to be in the public sector. However, the status of housing associations—independent bodies regulated by the state and commonly in receipt of public funding—continues to change.[3] Housing provides a good example of the way in which very similar public interest issues can arise in both private and public sector contexts. Both council housing and housing associations are within the jurisdiction of the PSOs in Northern Ireland, Scotland, and Wales and the joint PHSO and LGSCO response to the draft Bill considered that responsibility for housing complaints should be included within the jurisdiction of the new PSO from the start. As noted below, the arguments for including housing within an integrated PSO appear to be strong.

What does this mean for legislative reform? The first principle is that there should be acknowledgment of the changing landscape for public

[3] English associations were removed from the national balance sheet in 2017 as the Office for National Statistics considered that there was no longer enough local or central government influence to keep them in the public sector. In *Weaver v London & Quadrant Housing Trust* [2009] EWCA Civ 235 the English High Court has ruled that not all housing associations are public authorities and not everything they do are public acts. The touchstone here is the nature of the act and how close to the State it approaches, with a view that housing associations could be subject to judicial review in certain circumstances.

service delivery and the increasing involvement of the private sector. The Venice Principles should be implemented by making explicit statutory provisions authorising the ombud to investigate private sector bodies whose services are funded (or part funded) by the public purse. The second principle is that a broader approach should be taken to the debate about integration, which goes beyond considering which of the classic public jurisdictions (central government, local government, health, and housing) should or should not be merged, but instead considers the issue in terms of the degree of public interest inherent in the particular sector. This would also be in line with the Venice Principles approach of bringing 'general interest' services within the ombud's jurisdiction and would allow the debate to move beyond the increasingly outdated and unhelpful distinctions between public and private.

Principle 1: *the ombud's jurisdiction should extend to private sector bodies where these are in receipt of public funds*
Principle 2: *debates about the scope of the ombud's jurisdiction should not be limited to outdated public-private distinctions, but instead consider the degree to which the public interest is at stake in a particular sector*

Territorial Scope—England, England and Wales, or UK?

Territorial boundaries provided a significant driver for ombuds integration in the devolved UK nations, specifically in response to the new constitutional contexts. The creation of smaller devolved jurisdictions, coherently mapped against defined national boundaries, provided the opportunity to rationalise and integrate public service jurisdictions. As will be discussed below, size was also a significant driver, as the arguments against multiple specialist jurisdictions are particularly strong in smaller jurisdictions featuring small numbers of complaints. Devolution, providing a moment of constitutional change and renewal, also gave an opportunity to tackle system level issues in the design of ombud schemes that usually are beyond the attention span of the busy legislative programme at Westminster.

In Scotland, the first of the nations in the UK to integrate ombuds functions, Zbíral et al. (2007) observed how devolution, in effect, created a new level of governance. One of the duties imposed on the Scottish Parliament was to provide for 'the investigation of certain complaints of maladministration made to its members and which relate to action taken by or on behalf of a member of the Scottish Executive or other office-holders in the Scottish Administration' (Scotland Act 1998, s.91(1)). Combining ombud schemes through the Scottish Public Services Ombudsman Act 2002 was the chosen means to fulfil this duty.

Public Administration Select Committee (PASC), in its consideration of the need for ombudsman reform, recognised that the division of power between the devolved governments and the UK Parliament presented a difficulty in providing England with a national ombud service (Cabinet Office 2015b: 39–41). Consideration was given to various options to address this problem.[4] A response from the then Scottish PSO cautioned against confusing the UK function of the UK Parliamentary Ombud with the role of an English PSO, saying that 'You have to make sure that you do not put the UK as part of an English Public Services Ombudsman'. Although a single PSO was selected as the preferred way forward, there are convincing arguments in favour of establishing two separate ombuds: one for public services delivered across the UK and one for those public services delivered in England-only. Elliott (2006: 98–102) advocated the adoption of this model, saying that it would have two principal benefits: allowing 'local' ombudsmanry (concerning such matters as local government, health, social housing and general England-only administration) to be integrated, whilst meanwhile reserving UK matters to the jurisdiction of the Parliamentary Ombudsman. There is merit in further debate relating to this 'two-ombuds' approach, with consideration given to how this has 'worked' elsewhere in the world. Albeit operating in the context of a federal constitution, rather than in the UK's distinctive asymmetric devolution model, a potential comparator is the Commonwealth Ombudsman in Australia which considers complaints about the actions of Australian Government agencies at a national level, while state ombuds consider administration at state level.

A knock on benefit of separating out English and UK-wide jurisdictions is that it would reduce the dominance of health cases in the Parliamentary

[4] Such as retaining a public service ombud for the UK, creating a separate ombud service just for England, or for one ombud to take on the UK function and report to all Parliaments and Assemblies.

Ombudsman's caseload: it is noted that 80% of the cases currently considered by the PHSO are about healthcare (Tyndall et al. 2018). Having a separate UK Parliamentary Ombudsman would allow more focus on the central government remit without being 'distracted' by health. It would also allow the Parliamentary Ombud to revert back to its original role and function as a distinctively Parliamentary Ombud. Whatever structure is agreed, it needs to have the flexibility to adjust to further changes to the devolution settlement, while at the same time respecting the current responsibilities of PSOs in the devolved administrations. The overall principle suggested here is that there needs to be respect for the devolution settlement and that the ombud's jurisdiction needs to match with the UK's current territorial constitution.

Principle 3*: the ombud's jurisdiction must take account of the devolution settlement, with a separate ombud overseeing UK-wide public services and those that are England-only.*

Remit—Specialist or Generalist?

Kirkham (2019) contends that PSOs should provide a universal service, saying that 'As a general rule, all public services should be overseen by a single ombudsman to avoid complexity from the perspective of the citizen, with a strong justification required for the exceptions'. In creating an English PSO, therefore, the question is whether it should cover all public services or whether specialist ombuds will still be required in some sectors. Current ombuds with a public service remit and an English presence are the PHSO, LGSCO, HOS, Office of the Independent Adjudicator for Higher Education in England and Wales (OIA), the UK Service Complaints Ombudsman for the Armed Forces (SCOAF), the Prisons and Probation Ombudsman, and the Independent Office for Police Conduct (IOPC). The general principle proposed in this chapter, following Kirkham's argument, is that the ombuds should have an integrated public service jurisdiction unless there are good reasons for specialism to be retained in a particular area. Such reasons might include: the degree of controversy attached to the jurisdiction; the seriousness of the issues arising in the jurisdiction; and the level of public interest involved.

Public Services That Should Fall Under an Integrated Ombud's Jurisdiction

This chapter argues that the following areas could be integrated within the new PSO's jurisdiction:

- Local government
- Social care
- Health
- Housing
- Higher education

Seneviratne (2002: ch.3) commented nearly twenty years ago that the legislative creation of public sector ombuds assumed that any publicly provided service would be the discrete responsibility of either central government, local government, or the National Health Service (NHS). She said at the time that this was no longer valid and that there were complaints which crossed these jurisdictional boundaries. There are strong arguments for the integrating the health and social care remits of the PHSO and LGSCO, not least because this reflects the reality of what is happening on the ground with the rise of new models of delivering health and social care (National Audit Office 2017).

As noted above, the public interest issues arising in relation to housing are very similar whether they arise in the public or private sector. It is unclear why recent reform proposals have continued to seek to treat housing separately from other English public service or why merging the PHSO and LGSCO's jurisdictions has been less controversial than integrating housing. It seems likely that this results from structural issues in relation to where the responsibility for housing policy sits within government and a lack of an integrated approach to policy in this area.

In relation to higher education, there is a strong contrast between Northern Ireland and Scotland, where universities come under the jurisdiction of an integrated public services ombud and England and Wales where a specialist ombud exists (Office of the Independent Adjudicator for Higher Education). This chapter suggests that the formation of the 'stand-alone' OIA has a historic explanation. It related to the prevailing context and if an English PSO had existed at the time of its formation, then the work of the OIA may well have come under the remit of this (and the Welsh) PSO. The recent extension of the OIA's jurisdiction to cover private universities does not argue against integration since, as with housing, there are strong overlaps between public and private provision here, and a significant public interest at stake.

There are three potential disadvantages of integration: the loss of sector-specific contacts and focus; the loss of sector-specific expertise; and the overshadowing of certain issues by others that are more 'important' (in volume or perceived seriousness of complaints). In order to combat these challenges, the ombud would need a strategy in place to maintain and develop specialism among staff, sector-specific outreach and communication strategies, and an organisational structure that reflects the broad shape of, and divisions between, the public services the ombud oversees.

One option by which this focus could be embedded in the new ombud scheme would be for it to be required by statute to have a separate internal ombud post for different specialisms. In essence, this was the solution proposed by the Cabinet Office in 2000 when it suggested that the new office could be operated through a collegiate structure. By this device, the 'Chief' Ombud would be under a reporting duty to account separately for the performance of its different jurisdictions and establish a separate unit within the organisation to deliver each listed jurisdiction. Even within such required structuring though, the Chief Ombud would be enabled, to a greater extent than is currently the case in the sector, to integrate and share the staff skills, resources, and intelligence collated by the larger integrated ombud scheme for the benefit of the organisation as a whole.

Public Services That Require the Retention of a Special Ombud

Certain public services will continue to require a specialist ombud. The factors that militate towards the retention of a separate jurisdiction include:

- the degree of controversy attached to the jurisdiction;
- the seriousness of the issues arising in the jurisdiction; *and*
- the level of public interest involved.

The particular areas where a specialist ombud should be retained include: police, prison and probations, and armed forces. These services are both highly specialised and involve the state at its most potentially intrusive and powerful in relation to the individual interests at stake and that may be complained about. The coercive power of the state in these areas and the potential for complaints to raise matters of the highest public interest (also potentially bringing into play the most serious interferences with human rights) justify standalone ombuds operating here.

Pragmatically, there are also good reasons for distinct ombuds based on the degree of controversy that might attach to oversight of these services. Stuhmcke (2016) has commented in relation to the New South Wales Ombudsman having police oversight, that recent parliamentary inquiries have confirmed a longstanding opinion that police oversight has always been problematic for both police and for ombuds. She relates how, at the Commonwealth level, the Australian Law Reform Commission recommended that police complaints be removed from the ombudsman's jurisdiction because of resource considerations and the serious nature of the complaints. The police jurisdiction here risked both overshadowing the other work of the ombud and miring it in controversies that prevented effectiveness in other areas.

Principle 4*: the general principle is that public interest services should fall within the jurisdiction of a single integrated ombud, unless there are good reasons for this not to happen.*
Principle 5: *good reasons for deciding that a specialist ombud jurisdiction should be retained include, the degree of controversy attached to the jurisdiction, the seriousness of the issues arising in the jurisdiction, and the level of public interest involved.*

Size

Size has been a significant concern in relation to integration. Kirkham and Martin (2014) note that the decision not to introduce a general PSO when the PHSO came into being partly reflected a widespread concern that the ombuds would struggle to handle the amount of complaints that would come the office's way. Conversely, Kirkham (2019) has commented (in relation to the formation of the Public Services Ombudsman for Wales), how in a country the size of Wales there was little sense in maintaining a series of individual ombud offices to deal with different sectors of government separately. Indeed, in the smaller devolved jurisdictions size arguments push towards integration.

In a larger jurisdiction, however, questions of size might give weight to arguments against integration. Creating an overly large, bureaucratic, and unwieldy ombud may present challenges. Certainly, there is a danger that ombuds that become large bureaucracies in themselves may struggle to deliver the ombud's particular 'humanising' approach to public services. O'Brien (2017) notes that size may be a factor in Western Europe, observing that other states which approach the size of the UK or even England (such as Germany and Italy) do not have national ombuds at all. Generally, the arguments in relation to economies of scale become less acute where separate ombuds attract large enough numbers of complaints.

In large jurisdictions, therefore, arguments around size may point in a different direction compared with smaller jurisdictions. In large jurisdictions, the benefits of economies of scale may be less pronounced because the bespoke schemes are already of a significant scale, and converse arguments around a unified ombud becoming too large and cumbersome may come into play instead. As noted above, it will be important to make sure that an ombud with an integrated jurisdiction maintains an appropriate internal structure, that recognises differences between public services and is able to maintain its sensitivity to local issues and the needs of different types of service users. An integrated jurisdiction needs to avoid a one-size-fits-all approach.

Principle 6: *questions of size provide stronger arguments for integration in smaller jurisdictions than they do in larger jurisdictions, with stand alone ombuds being more justifiable on size grounds in larger jurisdictions.*
Principle 7: *in larger jurisdictions, there is a danger that ombuds become too big, which should be mitigated through internal structures that maintain specialisms, and a sensitivity to local issues and the needs of different types of service users.*

Conclusion

This chapter has sought to provide a better understanding of the arguments around the ombud's jurisdiction and the degree to which current ombuds' jurisdictions should be integrated. In doing so, it has suggested that attention needs to be focused on four factors, including the type of jurisdiction (private, public, and public interest), the territorial scope of the services being overseen (UK, England, and England and Wales), the remit of the ombud (whether specialism is required), and finally size (whether size argues for or against integration). In considering these issues, the chapter has outlined a set of principles that should guide the legislative reform process.

Enunciation of these jurisdiction-based principles allow us to return to the government's proposals as set out in the draft Public Services Ombudsman Bill. As will be evident, when evaluated against these principles a number of weaknesses stand out in relation to the Bill's approach (at least insofar as questions of principle are concerned). The Bill is, for example, relatively unambitious in its proposals for integration and takes a narrow view of the public services that should be included in the ombud's jurisdiction. It also fails to future-proof itself by recognising the potential for the public interest to be a factor in the new PSO's jurisdiction rather than simply whether a service is strictly speaking publicly or privately delivered.

The Bill also fails to take account of the UK's devolution settlement. Keeping a UK-wide jurisdiction attached to a large English public services ombuds would be typical of the UK's pragmatic and often unprincipled approach to devolution and public service reform. However, reverting to a standalone Parliamentary Ombuds would have benefits both in providing a genuinely national ombudsman and in allowing a renewed focus on the ombud's parliamentary role and parliamentary remit. The relationship with Parliament and the idea of the ombud as a parliamentary ombud has perhaps been lost in the development of mass complaint handling and there is an opportunity for the ombud to reconnect with that original mission.

In conclusion, therefore, the current draft Public Services Ombudsman Bill has a number of weaknesses and in particular:

- fails to recognise the increasingly blurry lines between public and private service provision;
- does not recognise the current devolution settlement and the need for the ombud's jurisdiction to reflect this;
- takes an unprincipled and timid approach to integration; *and*
- fails to consider how specialism and sensitivity to different service user needs can be maintained within an integrated public service ombud.

These matters should be the focus of renewed attention when the next stage of legislative reform arrives.

References

Bondy, V., & Le Sueur, A. (2012). *Designing Redress: A Study About Grievances Against Public Bodies*. London: Public Law Project.

Cabinet Office. (2010). *New Ombudsman Schemes: Guidance for Government Departments on Setting Up Ombudsman Schemes*. Retrieved November 8, 2019, from https://www.gov.uk/government/publications/new-ombudsman-schemes-guidance.

Cabinet Office. (2015a). *A Public Service Ombudsman: A Consultation*. Retrieved November 8, 2019, from https://assets.publishing.service.gov.uk/government/uploads/system/uploads/attachment_data/file/417111/Ombudsman_Service_Consultation.pdf.

Cabinet Office. (2015b). *A Public Service Ombudsman Government Response to Consultation*. Retrieved November 8, 2019, from https://assets.publishing.service.gov.uk/government/uploads/system/uploads/attachment_data/file/486797/PSO_-_Consultation_Response_-_Final.pdf.

Council of Europe. (2019). *Principles on the Protection and Promotion of the Ombudsman Institution* ("The Venice Principles"), adopted by the Venice Commission at Its 118th Plenary Session (Venice, 15–16 March 2019). Retrieved November 8, 2019, from https://www.venice.coe.int/webforms/documents/?pdf=CDL-AD(2019)005-e.

Elliott, M. (2006). Asymmetric Devolution and Ombudsman Reform in England. *Public Law*, 84–105.

Financial Ombudsman Service. (2000). *First Annual Report: Laying the Foundations*. Retrieved November 8, 2019, from https://www.financial-ombudsman.org.uk/files/2005/ar-1999-2000.pdf.

Gill, C., Creutzfeldt, N., Williams, J., & Vivian, N. (2017). Confusion, Gaps and Overlaps. Retrieved November 8, 2019, from https://www.citizensadvice.org.uk/about-us/policy/policy-research-topics/consumer-policy-research/consumer-policy-research/confusion-gaps-and-overlaps/.

Gordon, R. (2014). *Better to Serve the Public: Proposals to Restructure, Reform, Renew and Reinvigorate Public Services Ombudsmen*. Retrieved November 8, 2019, from https://assets.publishing.service.gov.uk/government/uploads/system/uploads/attachment_data/file/416656/Robert_Gordon_Review.pdf.

House of Commons Library. (2016). *Draft Public Service Ombudsman Bill*. Briefing Paper CBP 07864. Retrieved November 8, 2019, from https://researchbriefings.parliament.uk/ResearchBriefing/Summary/CBP-7864#fullreport.

International Ombudsman Institute. (2017). *Developing and Reforming Ombudsman Institutions*. Retrieved November 8, 2019, from https://www.theioi.org/publications/ioi-best-practice-papers.

Jersey Law Commission. (2018). *Designing a Public Services Ombudsman for Jersey*. Retrieved November 7, 2019, from https://jerseylawcommission.files.wordpress.com/2018/11/jsylawcom_designingombudsman_final.pdf.

Kirkham, R. (2019). A Manifesto for Legislative Reform of the Ombudsman Sector. Retrieved November 8, 2019, from https://ukaji.org/2019/03/28/a-manifesto-for-legislative-reform-of-the-ombudsman-sector/#comments.

Kirkham, R., & Martin, J. (2014). Designing an English Public Services Ombudsman. *Journal of Social Welfare and Family Law, 36*(3), 330–348.

National Audit Office. (2017). Health and Social Care Integration. Retrieved November 13, 2019, from https://www.nao.org.uk/wp-content/uploads/2017/02/Health-and-social-care-integration.pdf.

O'Brien, N. (2017). *No End of Searching: A Comment on the Draft Public Service Ombudsman*. Bill 2016. Retrieved November 8, 2019, from https://ukaji.org/2017/02/02/no-end-of-searching-a-comment-on-the-draft-public-service-ombudsman-bill-2016/#comments.

Ombudsman Services. (2018, January–December). *Ombudsman Services Annual Report*. Retrieved November 8, 2019, from https://www.ombudsman-services.org/about-us/annual-reports.

PASC (Public Administration Select Committee). 2014a. *More Complaints, Please!* HC 229.

PASC (Public Administration Select Committee). 2014b. *Time for a People's Ombudsman Service*. HC 655.

Seneviratne, M. (2002). *Ombudsmen: Public Services and Administrative Justice*. London: Butterworths.

Seneviratne, M. (2006). A New Ombudsman for Wales. *Public Law*, 6–14.

Stuhmcke, A. (2012). The Evolution of the Classical Ombudsman: A View from the Antipodes. *International Journal of Public Law and Policy, 2*(1), 83–95.

Stuhmcke, A. (2016). Australian Ombudsmen: A Call to Take Care. *Federal Law Review, 44*(3), 531–556.

Tyndall, P., Mitchell, C., & Gill, C. (2018). *Value for Money Study: Report of the Independent Peer Review of the Parliamentary and Health Services Ombudsman*. Retrieved November 8, 2019, from https://www.ombudsman.org.uk/sites/default/files/Value_for_Money_report_final.pdf.

Zbíral, R., Peterková, M., Horáková, M., Bartoň, M., Malacka, M., Tomoszková, V., & Tomoszek, M. (2007). *Devolution as an Impetus for Reform? The Case of the Scottish Ombudsman*. Retrieved November 8, 2019, from https://ssrn.com/abstract=2081935.

CHAPTER 5

The Ombud and Own-Initiative Investigation Powers

Chris Gill

Abstract This chapter argues that the ombud should be granted own-initiative powers of investigation. The case for this is four-fold: prevalence and successful experiences internationally; evidence in relation to complaining behaviour and the non-emergence of disputes; evidence in relation to under-representation of vulnerable groups; and identification of clear added-value contributions arising from own-initiative powers. The chapter explores how own-initiative powers should be calibrated and framed. International practice is analysed on investigation triggers, criteria for launching investigations and topics commonly investigated. The chapter considers three arguments against own-initiative powers—the "red-tape", "mission drift" and "rogue ombud" arguments—and suggests that each of these can be answered through appropriate legislative framing. The chapter concludes that broad powers are required, controlled through reporting requirements that balance accountability and effectiveness.

Keyword Own-initiative investigation • Ombuds • International ombud practice • Ombud overreach • Ombud accountability

C. Gill (✉)
University of Glasgow, Glasgow, UK
e-mail: Chris.Gill@glasgow.ac.uk

R. Kirkham, C. Gill (eds.), *A Manifesto for Ombudsman Reform*,
https://doi.org/10.1007/978-3-030-40612-7_5

Current UK Policy and Legislative Context

Prior to 2016, own-initiative powers of investigation were not available to ombuds in the UK. The situation has now changed, with first the Northern Ireland Public Services Ombudsman (Public Services Ombudsman (Northern Ireland) Act 2016 ss.8–9, s.29) and then the Public Services Ombudsman for Wales (Public Services Ombudsman (Wales) Act, ss. 4–5, 16) being granted own-initiative powers. Own-initiative powers are not available to the Scottish Public Services Ombudsman (Public Services Reform (Scotland) Act 2010) or to the Parliamentary and Health Services Ombudsman, and all English ombuds with a public service jurisdiction.[1]

The academic consensus has been that own-initiative powers of investigation would provide a valuable additional tool for UK ombuds (Harlow 1978, 2018; Lewis and Birkinshaw 1993; Buck et al. 2011; Gill 2012) and several authoritative reports have recently argued in favour of ombuds being granted these powers (Jersey Law Commission 2018; Guerin et al. 2018). The parliamentary committee responsible for overseeing the Parliamentary and Health Services Ombudsman has also consistently advocated own-initiative powers.[2] The government's response to that committee's most recent recommendation regarding own-initiative powers, in 2014, was to commission Robert Gordon to conduct an independent review while being cautiously welcoming of the proposal (PASC 2013–2014: 3).

The Gordon Review subsequently recommended the adoption of own-initiative powers subject to certain limitations (Gordon 2014). Gordon noted that previous recommendations for own-initiative powers were rejected due to fears that they would distract resources away from the investigation of individual complaints and because there were inadequate safeguards to control power being exercised by a single office holder. As a result, he recommended (subject to the proposals being "tested") that own-initiative powers should be accompanied by a number of safeguards such as a published statement on how investigations would be approached; documentation of the rationale, background and methodology of

[1] Including: the Health Service Ombudsman, the Local Government and Social Care Ombudsman, the Housing Ombudsman Service and the Office of the Independent Adjudicator for Higher Education.

[2] The committee recommended own-initiative powers in 1977, 1993 and 2014. For discussion, see Harlow (2018).

investigations; and notification of bodies proposed for investigation.[3] In its response to a subsequent consultation on the Gordon proposals, the government ruled out own-initiative powers because of the perceived risk that they could "detract from the PSO's [Public Services Ombud's] role in putting things right for the individual citizen" (Cabinet Office 2015).

The government's scepticism—mirrored in earlier rejections of the idea as "unnecessary and undesirable" (cited in Harlow 2018: 82)—reflects a wider unease in recent UK policy discussions with the potential for own-initiative powers to be abused. This is shown in the provisions enacted in Northern Ireland, which restrict the ombud to launching own-initiative investigations where the ombud has a "reasonable suspicion" that "there is systemic maladministration" or "systemic injustice" (Public Services Ombudsman (Northern Ireland) Act 2016, s.8). These provisions were enacted despite submissions from the Ombudsman Association and the International Ombudsman Institute which argued that the ombud should be granted broad discretion and that references to systemic maladministration and injustice were unduly narrow. The Welsh legislation is similarly cautious. It provides that: the ombud must be satisfied the investigation is in the public interest; a vulnerable or disadvantaged person is likely to sustain injustice or hardship as a result of the matter proposed for investigation; and/or the matter is likely to amount to a systemic failure that may cause a person injustice of hardship (Public Services Ombudsman (Wales) Act, s. 5).

The Case for Own-Initiative Powers

There are four sets of arguments in favour of granting the ombud own-initiative powers.

International Prevalence and Experience

The fact that own-initiative powers are widely used in other jurisdictions is not, in itself, an argument for adopting them in the UK. At the same time, the fact that they are widely used, with no significant concerns and some

[3] The Gordon Review proposed that a new Parliamentary Commission should be created to hold the ombudsman to account for its performance and to set its budget, while the role of the Public Administration and Constitutional Affairs Committee would be focused on using intelligence produced by the ombudsman to hold government departments to account.

evidence of success should—at the very least—lead to close scrutiny of any case for exceptionalism within the UK. Unfortunately, a comprehensive global study of own-initiative powers is not available. However, the International Ombudsman Institute has commissioned authoritative surveys of two regions (Europe and Australasia and Pacific) and found the powers to be widespread:

- Only 7 (15%) members of the Council of Europe (composed of 47 countries) do not currently have own-initiative powers (Northern Ireland Public Service Ombudsman 2014; Kucsko-Stadlmayer 2008).
- All jurisdictions in the Australasia and Pacific region have own-initiative powers (Frahm 2013).

In relation to the appropriate use and effectiveness of own-initiative powers, there is little systemic evidence and we have to rely largely on self-assessment by ombud practitioners. That said, there does not appear to be any widespread adverse commentary on these powers in the countries in which they exist and the International Ombudsman Institute has stated that: "there has not been any evidence to support the view that the own motion power has been used irresponsibly by members" (IOI 2015). Ombuds that possess own-initiative powers have tended to identify these as particularly important in securing the effectiveness of their offices (Passemiers et al. 2009). A recent best-practice paper published by the International Ombudsman Institute has argued that own-initiative powers can be "indispensable", providing a means of addressing emerging issues before they escalate, bringing matters of public interest to policymakers' attention, demonstrating the value of the office by providing tangible improvements to people's lives and allowing light to be shed on issues affecting people who are less likely to complain (IOI 2018: 3).

Complaining Behaviour

An important argument in favour of own-initiative powers concerns what we know about citizens' propensity to complain about public services. Only one in two people who experience a problem with a public service will complain, compared to nine in ten who will complain if they experience a problem with a bank (National Audit Office 2015). The effect of this is significant when we consider that 10.6 million citizens experienced a problem with a public service in 2016, meaning that around five million people had a problem for which they did not seek a remedy. Even for those who complain, the evidence is that most suffer from complaint fatigue and are unwilling to escalate issues to an ombud: only 27% of people who complain to a service provider and remain dissatisfied choose to take their complaint further (WHICH 2015). These statistics reflect longstanding evidence in the socio-legal literature that shows that there are numerous barriers to people taking action when they experience a problem.

The process through which a dispute emerges from a poor experience to an actual complaint has been famously described as involving three stages: naming, blaming and claiming (Felstiner et al 1980). Each of these stages includes barriers to a complaint being made. At the naming stage, people must be aware that they have had a bad experience—they may not know their legal rights or what level of service they are entitled to. At the blaming stage, people may know that they have had a problem, but not be sure of who to blame for it—it may be unclear who is at fault and how to frame a complaint, particularly where the issues or context of the dispute is complex. Finally, at the claiming stage, people may lack the resources (either financial, emotional or intellectual) to make a complaint and pursue it in an effective manner. There is, therefore, a significant likelihood of large scale un-remedied injustice within public services. As will be argued in Chap. 5, one approach to this problem is to improve complaint systems, but even with better complaint systems, own-initiative powers have the potential to play a special role in targeting areas where complaints are low, but problems are likely.

Vulnerable Groups

The problem of non-complaining behaviour is particularly acute for vulnerable groups and for groups who suffer discrimination and social injustice. Indeed, non-complainants are not representative of the general population and are more likely to be from particular demographic and socio-economic groups. For example, people who tend not to complain about public services are more likely to be young, male, black and minority ethnic, have disabilities and be unemployed (PHSO 2011: 35). Vulnerable groups are, therefore, less likely than others to benefit from the presence of complaint mechanisms and the ombud, making it highly likely that levels of un-remedied injustice are significantly higher here than among the general population. More perniciously, the fact that vulnerable groups are less likely to use complaint mechanisms has led to concern that public services are more likely to be distorted towards—or captured by—those who are most able to make effect use of complaint systems (Hastings and Matthews 2011). This has been a longstanding concern of ombud researchers, who have been concerned that ombuds tend to be used by a very narrow demographic and not to serve the interests of the socially excluded. This has been described as creating a "Matthew effect" where ombuds—formally designed to be equally accessible to everyone—in fact replicate and exacerbate social disadvantage because of disparities in propensity to complain (Hubeau 2018).

The implications of the evidence we have on who currently uses complaint and ombud systems leads to two conclusions: the current "reactive" approach of the ombud is, (a) at best, unlikely to cater effectively for those in society who may be most in need of securing justice, and (b) at worst, may be exacerbating disadvantage by guiding the attention of public services away from the excluded and towards the more vocal and powerful users of complaint systems. These conclusions provide good arguments in favour of granting the ombud own-initiative investigation powers, since such powers allow the ombud to target specifically those areas and groups from which complaints are less likely, providing justice for them and, potentially, helping to redress any distortive Matthew effects. The need for such powers has become more pressing following the managerial reforms of the last 40 years, which have sought to introduce greater choice in public service delivery and encourage citizens to behave as consumers (Hood and Dixon 2015). If the ombud is to act as a safeguard against injustice arising from the consumerisation of public services, it needs more tools at its disposal than it currently has.

Added Value

A final argument concerns the idea that own-initiative powers provide an opportunity to exploit the underdeveloped potential and distinctiveness of the ombud institution. Currently, the ombud's approach is predominantly that of a small claims court, dealing with large numbers of individual claims, occasionally grouping these together into big inquiries where multiple complaints are received about a particular issue. While the focus on the quality of administration already makes the ombud distinctive compared with courts and tribunals, its inquisitorial powers and theoretical ability to probe the administrative process in a much deeper way is currently limited. While there should be caution about making assumptions that the ombud is effective in improving administrative processes (Gill 2018), a current limitation is that the predominant legislative focus of the ombud is on individual injustice rather than a more general emphasis on bringing about good administration. This is argued to be a missed opportunity, with the ombud being insufficiently distinct within the administrative justice system (Harlow 2018). While some argue that own-initiative powers should be granted to the ombud as part of a radically recast role, where the ombud becomes an "inspector of public services" (ibid.: 88), they could also provide a useful addition to the existing ombud paradigm. Indeed, while maintaining the ombud's current role as an independent and final stage of public service complaint processes, there are opportunities for the ombud to deliver significant added value through the use of own-initiative powers.

What value would be added? One concern of government in resisting own-initiative powers relates to duplication, particularly where there are regulatory or inspection regimes already in operation. The first point to make here is that there is no general regulator of public services, and while some areas such as health and housing are subject to sectoral regulation, large swathes of public services are not subject to that type of oversight. As a result, an ombud empowered to consider more systemic matters would not necessarily be treading on the toes of other institutional actors. Secondly, even where regulators and other oversight bodies exist, the contribution of an ombud with own-initiative powers of investigation would be inherently distinct and bring a perspective to the administrative process that is beyond the expertise of regulators and others (Gill 2012). A more proactive role, including own-initiative powers, would be additional to regulatory approaches in a number of ways:

> There are three additional functions for ombudsmen …: (a) to provide a fully independent perspective, able critically to evaluate the performance of the regulatory regime as well as the regulated activity, (b) to allow for the ad hoc investigation of serious systemic matters arising outside of the regulator's routine inspection regimes, and (c) to go beyond narrow rules and, instead, champion the cause of good administration, thereby fulfilling what Buck et al. (2011) have referred to as a unique 'constitutional service'. (Gill 2012: 210)

More specifically, the unique contribution of the ombud's own-initiative powers would be an emphasis in investigations on:

- *The fairness of the administrative process.* While regulators are likely to be concerned with compliance, and auditors with the efficiency and effectiveness of performance, there is an ombud-shaped gap around the fairness and equity of administrative processes.
- *The quality of internal redress processes.* Ombudsmen in the UK have a longstanding interest and expertise in internal complaints processes and are well placed to secure improvements here. A quasi-regulatory model is advocated in Chap. 5, but own-initiative powers would allow for investigations where acute issues are apparent.

In addition to adding value to existing oversight bodies such as regulators, auditors and inspectors, an ombud with own-initiative powers would make a distinctive contribution to the administrative justice system. This is because neither courts nor tribunals have the institutional capacity and orientation to investigate issues proactively, even where it might appear that there is a need to do so. In this respect, there have been suggestions that an ombud with own-initiative powers could take on a more powerful role within the administrative justice system, not only investigating proactively to secure the ends of administrative justice but also fulfilling a wider range of systemic functions (Jersey Law Commission 2018). One of these would involve the ombud becoming a "system fixer" and "learning agent" for the administrative justice system, where the ombud's concern would be extended from complaints to administrative redress more generally:

> the ombudsman as learning agent would require new powers of own-initiative investigation, which could be harnessed to trouble-shoot problem areas within the administrative justice system. For example, the ombudsman might launch an investigation in areas where there are high levels of successful appeals, or in response to concerns raised in the annual reports of the Senior President of Tribunals. The ombudsman might also investigate where new initiatives have a significant knock on effect on the administrative justice system, such as currently in relation to mandatory reconsideration. There is also potential for the ombudsman to follow up individual cases. … Here, judges might refer cases to the ombudsman for follow up where public interest issues appear to be at stake. (Gill 2016: 349) [4]

[4] Proposals for more joint working between ombudsman offices and courts have previous been made by Lord Woolf in the 1990s, and more recently—in relation to ombudsman and offices and tribunals—by Sir Ernest Ryder.

International Evidence

This section of the chapter provides examples of the way in which the own-initiative powers have been used in other countries around the world. The aim is to provide some concrete examples to inform policy discussion of how own-initiative powers might be used in the UK.

Investigation Triggers

Own-initiative investigations can be prompted by information coming from various sources including: media reports, whistleblowing, parliamentary debates, referrals from other agencies and existing complaints to the ombud. In an analysis of the use of own-initiative investigations across nine countries around the world carried out by Diez, own-initiative powers seemed mostly to be used to broaden out investigations where an initial complaint had been received and in response to media reports (Diez 2018). Despite the limited range of information sources highlighted in Diez's study, the range of potential investigation triggers can be quite broad. The following list provides a fuller account of the potential triggers that might lead to an own-initiative investigation:

1. A complaint or series of complaints about a particular or similar issue;
2. The Ombudsman's perception of significant public concern about an issue;
3. The outcome of the Ombudsman's research on the issue;
4. A media report;
5. An organisation's own internal governance arrangements and external audit having highlighted an issue;
6. Report or reference from another oversight or integrity body;
7. Identified as a result of scrutiny by a Committee of the Legislature (Northern Ireland Ombudsman 2014).

It is interesting to note that despite this potential breadth of triggers, ombuds in many jurisdictions remain relatively complaint-driven in terms of their use of own-initiative powers. For example, the ombud in Ireland and in Ontario (Canada) both normally launch own-initiative investigations in order to pursue matters that have arisen from one or more complaints made to the ombud (Ibid.). This suggests that, in practice, the concern that granting own-initiative powers to ombuds distracts them from individual complaint handling may be overstated.

Investigation Criteria

The criteria for launching own-initiative investigations are variable across jurisdictions, although "as a rule, the ombudsman is provided with wide scope of discretion to conduct investigations *ex officio*" (Kucsko-Stadlmayer 2008: 21). In Europe, for example, there is a range of practice in relation to the circumstances in which an own-initiative investigation may be launched. At one end of the scale, as in Denmark, there is absolute discretion to investigate and no rationale need be given for launching an enquiry. Here, completed administrative proceedings are randomly checked. At the other end of the scale, the use of own-initiative powers is significantly restricted, as in Albania where the investigation can only be launched with the consent of the investigated party. In very limited cases, the subject matter of own-initiative investigations is constrained, for example, in Russia there is a requirement that the alleged actions to be investigated relate to gross violations of human rights, cases of special public significance, or be necessary to protect persons unable to access legal mechanisms. Most commonly, however, investigation criteria only require the suspicion or assumption that there has been maladministration.

In addition to formal legislative criteria which regulate the use of own-initiative powers, many ombuds have developed internal criteria in order to guide the use of their discretion. The Dutch National Ombudsman, for example, uses the following criteria to determine whether an own-initiative investigation should be launched:

- the size of the problem, that is, the number of complaints received, the number of people potentially affected and the potential advantage of bundling complaints;
- those affected, that is, vulnerable groups, minority groups and groups for whom the state has a special responsibility such as inmates or refugees;
- the type of problem, that is, gravity of the problem in terms of impact on people's lives, whether human rights are at stake, which norms of proper conduct are violated, the impact of the problem on people's trust in the authorities, whether Kafkaesque bureaucracy is involved;
- the value added of the ombudsman on this topic in relation to other institutions already addressing it, such as parliament, the court of auditors, non-governmental organisations (NGOs) and so on; and

- the timing of the investigation, in relation to people's increasing mistrust or societal unrest, in relation to the legislative agenda or major political events (De Langen et al. 2018: 379).[5]

Investigation Topics

As noted above, one of the governmental concerns with regard to own-initiative powers appears to be that they could be misused. Tables 5.1 and 5.2 below provide some illustrative examples of the kinds of issues that have been subject to own-initiative investigations in order to provide a clearer sense of what kind of added value might be delivered (Diez 2018).[6] Table 5.1 provides examples of where an own-initiative investigation concerns an issue of general public interest, whose resolution has the potential to affect large numbers of people.

Table 5.2 below provides examples of own-initiative investigations launched in order to protect vulnerable and disadvantaged groups.[7]

Table 5.1 Examples of investigations into matters of general public interest

Ombudsman office	*Example of own-initiative topic*
European Ombudsman	Investigation into the transparency of lobbying of the European Commission. Investigation focused on the composition and potential conflict of interests of expert groups set up to advise the Commission.
Australian Ombudsman	Investigation into a Tourist Refund Scheme, which imposed a rule whereby refund claims had to be submitted at least 30 minutes before a flight's scheduled departure time. Investigation focused on the lawfulness of the 30 minute rule.
Peruvian Ombudsman	Investigation into the school admissions system, focusing on whether enrolment was conditional on paying a fee to join a parent's association; technical problems affecting enrolment; and inadequacies in the schools' estate.
Spanish Ombudsman	Investigation launched following a report by a charity that 50% of people who needed palliative care were not receiving it. Investigation focused on resources available for palliative care and variations in provisions.

[5] For the approach used in Ontario, Canada, see Jones (2009).
[6] The examples in the table are drawn from Diez (2018).
[7] Again the examples in the table are from Diez (2018).

Table 5.2 Examples of own-initiative investigation concerning vulnerable groups

Ombudsman office	*Example of own-initiative topic*
Costa Rican Ombudsman	Investigation launched into whether the healthcare system appropriately catered for people of African descent who had particular health needs.
Catalonian Ombudsman	Investigation into the management of waiting lists for allocating residential services for elderly people and people with disabilities.
Austrian Ombudsman	Investigation into the treatment of migrants who are minors and the way in which unaccompanied minor refugees were treated by state authorities.
Spanish Ombudsman	Investigation into the treatment of elderly people in prison and the lack of programmes particularly targeting this group.

Controlling Own-Initiative Powers

As noted above, despite recent developments in Northern Ireland and Wales, there has been a degree of scepticism of own-initiative powers in the UK. Assuming that own-initiative powers are granted, therefore, the next question is what form they should take and how far any statutory provisions should seek to constrain the ombud's discretion. There are three arguments against own-initiative powers:

- *The red tape argument*: there is the potential for overlap and duplication with other bodies;
- *The mission drift argument*: there is a potential loss of focus on individual complainants; *and*
- *The rogue ombud argument*: there is a potential for discretionary power to be abused by officer holders.

Red Tape Argument

The "red tape" argument has already been dealt with under section (c) (iv) above and the idea that there is duplication is misconceived, because: many areas of public service are not regulated; and even where other oversight actors exist they have a fundamentally different focus. The ombud's focus on fairness and on redress provides it with a unique locus of action which does not duplicate that of other institutional actors. That said, there is clearly a risk of confusion if multiple actors are investigating similar issues at the same time. As a result, it makes sense for the own-initiative power to be made subject to consultation with relevant stakeholders. The Public Services Ombudsman (Wales) Act, for example, in s. 4(3) provides that "the ombudsman must consult such persons as the Ombudsman considers appropriate when making such a decision [to launch an own-initiative investigation]". As a matter of good practice, the ombud might be expected to develop existing memoranda of understanding with key organisations in order to clarify how the ombud will consult stakeholders in practice.

Mission Drift Argument

There is some evidence to support this argument in research conducted in Australia. In an analysis of decision-making by the Commonwealth Ombudsman between 1977 and 2005, the ombud's use of discretion to not investigate complaints increased from 19% of cases in 1977 to 73% of cases in 2005. This shows the way in which—despite the legislative mandate of the ombud not changing—office-holders used their discretion to shift the focus towards more systemic work, while increasingly declining to investigate individual complaints. While this research has no direct bearing on the UK, it illustrates the potential danger inherent in granting the ombud powers that would push the ombud towards a more systemic role. While this danger exists, it should not be overstated. First, even without own-initiative powers, ombuds could use their discretion to adopt a more systemic outlook (e.g. putting more resources into "big cases", declining to investigate where the issue complained of falls below a certain level of seriousness, advertising for complaints in areas where systemic issues are suspected). Second, the ombud's use of discretion would continue to be subject to oversight by Parliament through the Public Administration and Constitutional Affairs Committee (or to a Public Ombud Commission if that proposal were to be adopted).

It should also be noted that there is a longstanding debate over whether "mission drift" would—at least to some extent—be beneficial. As argued in section (c) above, expanding the ombud's mission to assist non-complainants and vulnerable groups, as well as providing a more powerful means of tackling government maladministration and improving redress, are likely to provide a more modern and holistic mission for the ombud. While some argue that there is a need to be careful not to lose sight of the individual (Stuhmcke 2010: 143), others argue that it is not realistic for the ombud to continue to act as a small claims court for all public sector disputes (Harlow 2018). Indeed, there have been arguments from both independent reviews and academics, for the ombud's complaint investigation role to be largely removed, with investigations only focused on systemic matters or failures in the system of public service redress (Crerar 2007; Harlow 2018). The point is that—unlike the red tape argument or the rogue ombud argument, where there is more likely to be consensus about the need for measures to be taken—there is a broader argument to be had about whether mission drift is a good or a bad thing.

Rogue Ombud Argument

To prevent the abuse of the ombud's discretion to launch own-initiative investigations, two safeguards are required:

- Non-statutory criteria for launching own-initiative investigations should be published by the ombud and subject to approval by the Public Administration and Constitutional Affairs Committee, and thereafter be subject to periodic review.
- Annual reports should be made to the Public Ombud Commission (or Public Administration and Constitutional Affairs Committee [PACAC] if it retains responsibility for overseeing the ombud) detailing: the rationale for launching own-initiative investigations, the way in which the non-statutory criteria were applied, whether objections were received from the investigated party or other stakeholders, the ombud's response to those objections and the outcomes of investigations.

Requiring the publication and approval of investigation criteria and annual reporting of the way these have been applied provide for transparency and the opportunity to assess the quality of the ombud's decision-making. This ensures the right balance between giving the ombud broad discretion to make use of his or her powers, while guarding against any risk that powers will be misused.

Conclusion

This chapter has argued that the ombud currently serves a small and unrepresentative demographic, with the effect that (a) at best, vulnerable groups are not served well by the ombud and (b) at worst, vulnerable groups in fact suffer from a diversion of resources towards more vocal and powerful citizens. More generally, one in two people do not complain when something goes wrong and many more people may not even realise that they have cause to complain, which suggests that the current complaint-driven approach of the ombud is failing to deal with large scale un-remedied injustice. Consequently, this chapter argues that the ombud should be granted own-initiative powers, in order to allow the ombud to add value in the following ways:

- Addressing issues which are not complained about, as a result of a generally low propensity to complain;
- Addressing issues which affect particularly vulnerable groups, which are especially unlikely to come to light through complaints;
- Addressing matters of general public interest, which concern the fairness of administration, and are generally not the principal focus of other oversight bodies; *and*
- Addressing and having a special responsibility for the operation of redress systems and taking on a broader "system fixing" role within the administrative justice system.

This chapter has argued that the ombud should not be unduly constrained in the way the powers are framed. Instead, effectiveness requires that they should be granted in broad terms rather than being subject to unnecessary statutory constraints. Safeguards should be limited to ensuring that principles for investigation are drawn up by the ombud and approved by PACAC and that the use of own-initiative powers is regularly reported on and overseen by PACAC (or whichever body holds the ombud to account in future). Broad powers accompanied by proportionate oversight arrangements provide the best means of ensuring both effectiveness and accountability.

References

Buck, T., Kirkham, R., & Thompson, B. (2011). *The Ombudsman Enterprise and Administrative Justice*. Surrey: Ashgate.

Cabinet Office. (2015). *A Public Service Ombudsman Government Response to Consultation*. Retrieved November 7, 2019, from https://assets.publishing.service.gov.uk/government/uploads/system/uploads/attachment_data/file/486797/PSO_-_Consultation_Response_-_Final.pdf.

Crerar, L. (2007). *The Independent Review of Audit, Regulation, Inspection and Complaint Handling of Public Services in Scotland*. Edinburgh: Scottish Government.

De Langen, M., Govers, E., & Van Zutphen, R. (2018). Effectiveness and Independence of the Ombudsman's Own-Motion Investigations: A Practitioner's Perspective from the Netherlands. In M. Hertogh & R. Kirkham (Eds.), *Research Handbook on The Ombudsman*. Cheltenham: Edward Elgar.

Diez, L. (2018). The Use of Own-Initiative Powers by the Ombudsman. In M. Hertogh & R. Kirkham (Eds.), *Research Handbook on The Ombudsman*. Cheltenham: Edward Elgar.

Felstiner, W. L., Abel, R. L., & Sarat, A. (1980). The Emergence and Transformation of Disputes: Naming, Blaming, Claiming… *Law and Society Review*, 631–654.

Frahm, M. (2013). *Australasia and Pacific Ombudsman Institutions: Mandates, Competences and Good Practice*. New York: Springer.

Gill, C. (2012). The Impact of the Scottish Public Services Ombudsman on Administrative Decision-Making in Local Authority Housing Departments. *Journal of Social Welfare and Family Law, 34*(2), 197–217.

Gill, C. (2016). *Administrative Justice and the Control of Bureaucratic Decision Making*. University of Glasgow, Ph.D. thesis. Retrieved November 7, 2019, from http://theses.gla.ac.uk/7714/1/2016GillPhD.pdf.

Gill, C. (2018). What Can Government Learn from the Ombudsman? In M. Hertogh & R. Kirkham (Eds.), *Research Handbook on The Ombudsman*. Cheltenham: Edward Elgar.

Gordon, R. (2014). *Better to Serve the Public: Proposals to Restructure, Reform, Renew and Reinvigorate Public Services Ombudsmen*. Retrieved November 7, 2019, from https://assets.publishing.service.gov.uk/government/uploads/system/uploads/attachment_data/file/416656/Robert_Gordon_Review.pdf.

Guerin, B., McCrae, J., & Shepheard, M. (2018). *Accountability in Modern Government: Recommendations for Change*. Retrieved November 7, 2019, from https://www.instituteforgovernment.org.uk/sites/default/files/publications/Accountability_modern_government_WEB.pdf.

Harlow, C. (1978). Ombudsmen in Search of a Role. *Modern Law Review, 41*(4), 446–454.

Harlow, C. (2018). Ombudsmen: 'Hunting Lions' or 'Swatting Flies'. In M. Hertogh & R. Kirkham (Eds.), *Research Handbook on The Ombudsman*. Cheltenham: Edward Elgar.

Hastings, A., & Matthews, P. (2011). *"Sharp Elbows": Do the Middle-Classes Have Advantages in Public Service Provision and if So How?* Project Report. University of Glasgow, Glasgow, UK.

Hood, C., & Dixon, R. (2015). *A Government That Worked Better and Cost Less?* Oxford: OUP.

Hubeau, B. (2018). The Profile of Complainants: How to Overcome the Matthew Effect? In M. Hertogh & R. Kirkham (Eds.), *Research Handbook on The Ombudsman*. Cheltenham: Edward Elgar.

International Ombudsman Institute. (2018). *Own Initiative Investigations*. IOI Best Practice Paper, Issue 3.

IOI (International Ombudsman Institute). (2015). *IOI Submission to Ad Hoc Committee Established to Scrutinise NIPSO Bill*. Retrieved November 7, 2019, from http://www.niassembly.gov.uk/globalassets/documents/ad-hoc-nipso/submissions/11.international-ombudsman-institute.pdf.

Jersey Law Commission. (2018). *Designing a Public Services Ombudsman for Jersey*. Retrieved November 7, 2019, from https://jerseylawcommission.files.wordpress.com/2018/11/jsylawcom_designingombudsman_final.pdf.

Jones, G. (2009). *Conducting Administrative, Oversight and Ombudsman Investigations*. Ontario: Canada Law Book.

Kucsko-Stadlmayer, G. (Ed.). (2008). *European Ombudsman-Institutions. A Comparative Legal Analysis Regarding the Multifaceted Realisation of an Idea*. New York: Springer.

Lewis, N., & Birkinshaw, P. (1993). *When Citizens Complain: Reforming Justice and Administration*. Open University Press.

National Audit Office. (2015). *Public Service Markets: Putting Things Right When They Go Wrong*. Retrieved November 7, 2019, from https://www.nao.org.uk/wp-content/uploads/2015/06/Putting-things-right.pdf.

Northern Ireland Public Service Ombudsman. (2014). *A Paper Prepared by the Office of the Northern Ireland Ombudsman on a Power to Commence an Own Initiative Investigation*. Submission to the Welsh Assembly Finance Committee (January 2014).

PASC. (2013–2014). *More Complaints Please! and Time for a People's Ombudsman Service: Government Responses to the Committee's Twelfth and Fourteenth Reports of Session 2013–14*, HC 618.

Passemiers, R., Reynaert, H., & Steyvers, K. (Eds.). (2009). *The Impact of Ombudsmen*. Brugge: Vanden Broele Publishers.

PHSO (Parliamentary and Health Services Ombudsman) (2011). *Review of Government Complaint Handling 2011*. Retrieved November 7, 2019, from https://www.ombudsman.org.uk/sites/default/files/Responsive_and_accountable_parliamentary_report_2011-12_0.pdf.

Stuhmcke, A. (2010). Each for Themselves or One for All-The Changing Emphasis of the Commonwealth Ombudsman. *Federal Law Review, 38*, 143.
WHICH. (2015). *Make Complaints Count.* Retrieved November 7, 2019, from https://www.staticwhich.co.uk/documents/pdf/make-complaints-count-report%2D%2D-march-2015-397971.pdf.

CHAPTER 6

The Ombud and 'Complaint Standards Authority' Powers

Chris Gill

Abstract This chapter argues that the ombud should be granted Complaint Standards Authority (CSA) powers. It begins by defining these powers, since they represent a recent innovation, confined to the devolved jurisdictions of the UK. The chapter then makes a case for the adoption of CSA powers based on three arguments: evidence shows that problems within public service complaint systems are acute and urgent; the scale of these problems means that formal intervention is likely to be required; and the ombud is best placed in terms of expertise to address these issues. The chapter ends by considering arguments against CSA powers and concludes that these can be mitigated, particularly if the vision of a more powerful and conceptually coherent ombud, recommended in this book, is accepted.

Keyword Complaint standards authority • Ombuds • Devolution • Ombud overreach • Ombud accountability

C. Gill (✉)
University of Glasgow, Glasgow, UK
e-mail: Chris.Gill@glasgow.ac.uk

R. Kirkham, C. Gill (eds.), *A Manifesto for Ombudsman Reform*,
https://doi.org/10.1007/978-3-030-40612-7_6

Definition

The genesis of the Complaint Standards Authority powers can be found in Lorne Crerar's *Independent Review of Regulation, Audit, Inspection, and Complaint Handling of Public Services in Scotland*. Among other things, the Crerar Review recommended that:

> the SPSO is given a wider remit, in terms of designing systems which will make it easier to make complaints and which will ensure that outcomes are more closely linked to service improvements. (Crerar 2007: 10)

The subsequent group set up by the Scottish Government to consider Crerar's recommendations—the Fit-for-purpose Complaint System Action Group—coined the term 'design authority' to describe this new remit (Sinclair 2008: 8). The 'design authority' powers were subsequently translated into legislative provisions through s. 119 of the Public Services Reform (Scotland) Act 2010, which amended the Scottish Public Services Ombudsman Act 2002. These provisions include:

- New duties to:
  - publish a statement of complaint handling principles;
  - monitor practice and identify trends in how public bodies handle complaints;
  - promote best practice in complaint handling; *and*
  - encourage cooperation and sharing of best practice amongst public bodies.
- New powers to:
  - publish model complaint handling procedures for public bodies; *and*
  - issue a declaration of non-compliance where a complaints procedure does not conform to a model complaint handling procedure.

The Scottish Public Services Ombudsman (SPSO) implemented this new remit by creating what it called the Complaint Standards Authority, a small internal unit within the SPSO (SPSO 2009–2010: 3). The Complaint Standards Authority has been described as a function that is 'quasi-regulatory' (Gill 2014), that involves 'monitoring' rather than regulation,[1] and most recently as one combining 'developmental' work and 'oversight' (SPSO 2018: 4). While there are some questions over the exact delineation of the Complaints Standards Authority role (Gill et al. 2020), it basically involves a combination of standard-setting, monitoring and compliance checking, and promotion of good practice.

Current UK Policy Context

The Complaints Standards Authority model has been replicated in Northern Ireland, although the relevant provisions have yet to be brought into force (Public Services Ombudsman (Northern Ireland) Act 2016, ss. 34–42). The Public Service Ombudsman (Wales) Act also grants these powers to the Public Services Ombudsman for Wales. In relation to the Parliamentary and Health Services Ombudsman (PHSO), the Gordon Review considered whether the ombud should be granted similar powers. Its conclusions were broadly in favour of the Complaints Standards Authority approach, albeit laying more emphasis on the developmental rather than the quasi-regulatory aspects of the role and leaving open the question of whether a role in improving complaints handling should be put on a statutory footing. The UK Government's subsequent Draft Public Services Ombudsman Bill proposes a duty on the ombud to publish information, advice, and training for public bodies, and a duty on public bodies to have regard to such advice in their complaint handling arrangements. The role envisaged in the draft Bill, therefore, is very much as a promoter of best practice rather than an authority with formal standard-setting, monitoring, and compliance powers.[2]

The Case for the Complaint Standards Authority Role

The Crerar Review provides a useful starting point for understanding the case for the ombud to take on a more strategic and regulatory role in relation to public services complaint handling. It provided the following

[1] An SPSO interviewee cited in Mullen et al. (2017).

[2] It should be noted that SPSO's compliance powers are limited to issuing a declaration of non-compliance to the Scottish Parliament. In keeping with other aspects of the ombudsman's role, therefore, the idea is that non-compliance should have political rather than legal ramifications for public bodies.

analysis of the state of public services complaint handling in Scotland at the time:

- An overly complex system, with too much variation in terms of how complaints were dealt with, reported against, and externally scrutinised;
- A system that was confusing and very difficult for complainants to navigate, with procedures that were slow, expensive, time-consuming, and not meeting citizens' needs; *and*
- A system that did not consistently use complaints in order to improve services (Crerar 2007: paras. 11.4–11.10).

This analysis of public service complaint systems has been echoed in a number of other contexts. In studies conducted in 2005 (and updated in 2010), researchers found that the cost of providing redress in UK central government amounted to £1.5 billion a year and, overall, provided a 'lousy service at high cost' (Dunleavy et al. 2010: 421–56). Their conclusions were that redress processes required a PhD in public administration to understand, were slow moving, paper-bound, and ineffective, and there were strong variations in how data on complaints were collected and used. The overall conclusion of these studies was that the present system did not provide value for money and that the recommendations of the Crerar Review around simplification and streamlining of complaint processes should apply UK-wide.

The Public Administration Select Committee (PASC, now Public Administration and Constitutional Affairs Committee [PACAC]) has been concerned on an ongoing basis with the quality of complaint handling within public services. Its 2008 report, *When Citizens Complain*, concluded among other things that: there were systemic problems with government complaint handling; complaint systems were difficult to navigate; and government organisations were not actively monitoring and learning from complaints (PASC 2008). In PASC's 2013 report, *More Complaints Please!*, it noted that there were some signs of improvement but that:

> Government as a whole cannot be said to be complying with best practice in complaints handling or adapting to the needs and expectations of today's citizen. (PASC 2013–2014: 4)

In particular sectors—such as health—there have also been acute problems in relation to complaint handling. The Francis Report and the Clwyd-Hart Report both found a culture of denial on the part of health services, a reluctance by citizens to complain, and a failure on the part of services to address concerns that were raised (Francis 2013; Clwyd and Hart 2013).

Most recently, the National Audit Office's research found that complaints systems were overly complex and discouraged people to raise complaints; it found five key problems in the current complaint handling system:

- People not knowing who to complain to;
- Difficulties in raising complaints;
- Navigating the system once a complaint has been raised;
- Lack of timeliness in obtaining redress; *and*
- Gaps in the system (NAO 2015).

Research conducted by WHICH has found that when people do complain they are very unlikely to be satisfied with their experiences:

- Only 31% of people were satisfied with the outcome of their complaints;
- 48% felt their complaint had been ignored;
- 44% felt angry about how the complaint had been dealt with;
- 33% wished they had not bothered complaining;
- 46% felt that complaining had made their experience more stressful; *and*
- 26% said they were put off complaining again (WHICH 2015: 12–13).

Research conducted by the PHSO found similar problems among those who had used public service complaint procedures:

- 36% did not feel listened to;
- 57% were not kept up to date;
- 46% felt their complaint was not taken seriously; *and*
- 64% felt that their complaint would not make a difference (PHSO 2011: 35).

In relation to whether complaints make a difference, despite evidence of good practice and innovation in some areas (Simmons and Brennan 2017), the overall picture is that little use is made of complaints to improve services. The National Audit Office has found 'significant impediments to using complaints data for service improvement' including:

- A lack of systemic leadership;
- Complaints data and powers to enable improvement that are fragmented; *and*
- Little innovation in the analysis of consumer data (NAO 2015: 37).

The above discussion, therefore, suggests that there are very significant problems in the design and operation of public service complaints systems. Currently, these systems are overly complex and off-putting for citizens and—even where they are used by citizens—the evidence is that they do not meet their needs and expectations. Despite some evidence of learning from complaints, public services are not currently making good use of complaints as sources of data for improvement. The National Audit Office (NAO)'s conclusions on the need for change are clear:

> If government took the power of redress to improve public services seriously, it would recognize that the present system is incoherent and dissatisfying to users and would show urgency in reforming and rationalizing the system. (Morse 2015)

While the problems with public service complaint handling are clear, and there is extensive evidence to support the need for change of some sort, a question remains about whether the best policy solution is to give further powers to the ombud. There are of course alternative approaches that may be adopted:

- Issuing non-statutory guidance and advice (perhaps along the lines of a renewed Citizens Charter programme with its Complaint Handling Taskforce) (see Blackmore 1997);
- Providing the National Audit Office (and sectoral regulators) with a particular responsibility for the routine oversight and performance monitoring of complaint handling processes;
- If Complaints Standards Authority-like powers are felt to be required, giving them to a body other than the ombud, for example:
  - Creating a new body;

- Providing similar powers to an existing cross-governmental body (e.g. the Cabinet Office, with its powers of coordination across government);
- Providing similar powers to other oversight bodies such as regulators or inspectors, who would be responsible for complaint handling in particular sectors (e.g. the Care Quality Commission in the health sector).

Each of these options would, however, be unsatisfactory. While non-statutory guidance and advice can be effective, the large-scale problems of system design that need to be tackled require an authoritative, centralised, and directive approach. It is noteworthy in this respect that there already exists a significant amount of guidance for public bodies in relation to the design and operation of complaint systems.[3] The problem is not so much the availability of guidance, as a failure by public service providers to prioritise complaint handling and to align existing approaches with best practice. Consequently, more guidance is unlikely to provide the step-change required given the problems in the current complaint handling landscape. Providing auditors and regulators with specific duties to monitor complaint handling should be considered, and such bodies may be better suited to a monitoring task than the ombud.[4] However, they would not be in a good position to act as standard-setters in relation to complaints, and do not have the expertise in complaint handling to advise on the design of complaints procedures or to facilitate and promote good practice in this area. An advantage of granting standard-setting, monitoring, and best practice promotion powers to a single body is that coherence and simplicity are more likely to be achieved. Whether such holistic Complaints Standards Authority powers could realistically be granted to a body other than the ombud is questionable. The creation of a new body is politically unlikely in the current financial climate. Few bodies have the kind of cross-governmental remit that could incorporate the role effectively and previous suggestions for a greater role by the Cabinet Office in relation to

[3] For example, Principles of Redress (Parliamentary and Health Services Ombudsman), Principles of Complaint Management (Ombudsman Association), Axioms of Good Administration (Local Government and Social Care Ombudsman), and Valuing Complaints (Scottish Public Services Ombudsman).

[4] In Scotland, the SPSO works in partnership with bodies such as Audit Scotland and expects monitoring of complaint handling to be a part of the activities of other oversight bodies rather than the sole responsibility of the ombudsman.

complaint handling (PASC 2013–2014) do not seem to have been particularly effective. Devolving responsibility to sectoral bodies has a superficial attraction but carries the risk that different approaches will be developed in different sectors and that the overall coherence of the complaint handling system will remain unaddressed.

Consequently, this chapter argues that:

- There are significant, acute problems in the UK's public service complaint handling system which require urgent reform;
- New standard-setting, monitoring, and best practice promotion powers are likely to be required given the scale of these problems; *and*
- The ombud is better placed than other bodies to take on these additional functions.[5]

Evidence from Scotland

The only evidence relating to the use of Complaints Standards Authority powers comes from Scotland, where this innovation originated.[6] The implementation of the Complaints Standards Authority there has not been formally evaluated and there is, therefore, a limited evidence base on which to draw. The Scottish Public Services Ombudsman's own assessment is that the powers are useful and are beginning to bring about positive change in the culture and practice of complaint handling in Scottish public services (PASC 2013–2014: 30). Indeed, it is clear that there has been considerable standardisation and simplification within Scottish public services, with most public bodies now operating a simple two stage process:

- Stage 1: early resolution (5 working days)
- Stage 2: investigation (20 working days)

This represents a major achievement and the system for public service handling in Scotland is now considerably more rational, simple, clear, and

[5] As will be argued below, there are some potential issues with the ombudsman taking on a new role which involves elements of redress regulation rather than the investigation of maladministration. Nonetheless, the chapter concludes, on balance, that the ombudsman remains best placed to address the systemic problems in public service complaint handling.

[6] Although these powers have been enacted for Northern Ireland, they have yet to be commenced.

coherent than that for UK and English public services. The SPSO has also developed and supported complaint handling networks in various sectors and produced a large amount of guidance and training resources to help improve complaint handling.[7] A small academic study found that local authority officials closely involved in the implementation of newly designed complaint procedures appear to consider that the new arrangements have been a success (Mullen et al. 2017). While recommending some small improvements in the detail of the scheme, this study suggested that there was scope for investigating whether a similar approach could be effective in other parts of the public sector. This conclusion should, however, be seen as a cautious one based on a limited evidence base. There has yet to be any assessment of whether these new procedures and guidance have led to changes for citizens; for example, whether they find it easier to complain, less confusing, quicker, and more worthwhile.[8] There is an obvious need for research here as the ultimate outcomes of the Complaints Standards Authority reforms remain largely unknown. That said, at least on the face of it, the simplification and coherence in the overall approach to complaint handling should be expected to be inherently beneficial to citizens.[9]

Potential Issues

Finally, we should note that there are some potential issues with granting Complaints Standards Authority powers to the ombud.

- *Mission drift and red tape.* The arguments discussed in Chap. 5 in relation to own-initiative investigations also apply here. Providing the ombud with quasi-regulatory standard-setting and monitoring powers may encourage the prioritisation of systemic goals over the interests of individuals with a complaint. There is also a danger that the imposition of more binding standards and reporting requirements encourages an overly bureaucratic approach to complaint

[7] See: http://www.valuingcomplaints.org.uk. Accessed 8 November 2019.

[8] Some concern has also been expressed that CSA powers have pushed the SPSO further towards a 'managerial' orientation that might be at odds with other administrative justice values. See Gill et al. (2020).

[9] One issue that requires further consideration relates to the fundamental philosophy, purpose, and practices of complaint systems. Providing the ombudsman with Complaints Standards Authority powers provides not only an opportunity to simplify and standardise but rethink the whole purpose and orientation of complaint systems. See Gill (2018).

handling, increasing red tape, while reducing creativity, flexibility, and responsiveness to citizens. Complaint handling standards may also require significant coordination with existing regulation and guidance produced by sectoral regulators, potentially duplicating efforts in some areas.

- *Constitutional blurring.* The ombud's current constitutional position remains a matter for debate; however, an argument can be made that providing the ombud with prospective regulatory functions (rather than largely retrospective powers of investigation) represents a significant shift in its role. In particular, the ombud's independence and its role as an impartial adjudicator of complaints could be compromised by entering into regulatory relationships with public bodies. Regulatory functions are generally executive functions, and while the UK's separation of powers is fluid, there is a danger that the ombud's distinctive position as a redresser of grievances (and part of the administrative justice system) gives way to a role as one of a number of regulators of public services (Gill 2014).
- *Relationship with public bodies.* The pragmatic consequences of a potential constitutional blurring might be reflected in the ombud's relationship with public bodies. In order to take on an expanded role of supporting best practice more dynamically and providing ongoing oversight, there will need to be a different approach compared with that of a detached and impartial adjudicator. The kind of dangers that face regulators in relation to 'capture' and the adoption of modern 'responsive' forms of regulation that use greater elements of soft power and negotiation, may bring the ombud into closer relationships with public bodies. These have the potential to improve outcomes since more cooperative approaches have been suggested as an important means of ensuring that public services learn from the ombud (Hertogh 2001). But there is also a risk that the ombud becomes seen by citizens as less impartial and more closely aligned to the interests of public bodies.
- *Capacity, skills, and scaling-up.* Taking on a more developmental approach on the one hand (advice, guidance, support) and a more regulatory approach on the other (standard-setting, performance monitoring, benchmarking) is likely to require different skills compared with complaint investigation. The ombud will therefore need

to invest in developing a new area of business.[10] The scale of the investment required is unclear and the greater scale of public service delivery in the UK/England means that the resources required will be significantly more than the modest resources deployed in Scotland. There is also perhaps a question mark over whether the approach that appears to have been successful in Scotland—involving high levels of cooperative working with sectoral complaint handling networks—could be replicated on a much larger scale.[11] Some of the ability to drive change in Scotland may also be reflected in cultural and structural differences in public service delivery in that jurisdiction.

While these issues represent important areas for further discussion and continued monitoring in relation to the Complaints Standards Authority function, the pressing need for improvements in public service complaint handling and the fact that the ombud is better placed than other bodies to take the lead mean that such issues do not—on balance—outweigh the potential benefits to be derived from giving the ombud additional powers.

Conclusion

This chapter has argued that there is extensive evidence of widespread and acute problems in public service complaint handling at a UK/England level. Complaint systems are currently confusing, inconsistent, incoherent, deliver poor outcomes for complainants, and are subject to low levels of public satisfaction. The options for addressing this situation include the development of non-statutory programmes, giving a greater role to regulators and auditors, and providing more of an emphasis on monitoring complaint handling by existing oversight regimes. Each of these approaches has potential limitations on its own, however, and an advantage of the Complaints Standards Authority approach is the fact that it provides holistic powers of standard-setting, monitoring and compliance, and best practice promotion to a single body with expertise in complaint handling.

[10] Steps are already being taken in this direction. Objective 3 of the PHSO's current strategic plan refers to developing the office's work to help support public bodies to handle complaints better. See PHSO (2018).

[11] Mullen, T., Gill, C. and Vivian, N. 2017. *Scotland's Model Complaint Handling Procedures: Exploring Recent Developments and the Usefulness of Complaint Data for Administrative Justice Research*. Project Report. University of Glasgow, Glasgow.

The chapter acknowledges that there is limited evidence with regard to the effectiveness of the Complaints Standards Authority approach in Scotland, although the evidence available and *prima facie* indications are that the approach should improve complaint handling and be of benefit to complainants and the wider public. There are also some issues attendant on the Complaints Standards Authority approach and its replication in a bigger jurisdiction; however, the chapter has argued that these are not insurmountable and that such an approach offers to best hope of tackling the very serious problems currently in evidence in relation to the UK/England's public service complaint systems.

References

Blackmore, M. (1997). Complaints Within Constraints: A Critical Review and Analysis of the Citizen's Charter Complaints Task Force. *Public Policy and Administration, 12*(3), 28–41.

Clwyd, A., & Hart, T. (2013). *A Review of the NHS Hospitals Complaints System*. Retrieved November 8, 2019, from https://assets.publishing.service.gov.uk/government/uploads/system/uploads/attachment_data/file/255615/NHS_complaints_accessible.pdf.

Crerar, L. (2007). *The Independent Review of Audit, Regulation, Inspection and Complaint Handling of Public Services in Scotland*. Edinburgh: Scottish Government.

Dunleavy, P., Bastow, S., Tinkler, J., Goldchluk, S., & Towers, E. (2010). Joining Up Citizen Redress in UK Central Government. In M. Adler (Ed.), *Administrative Justice in Context*. Oxford: Hart Publishing.

Francis, R. (2013). *Report of the Mid-Staffordshire NHS Foundation Trust Public Inquiry*. HC 947.

Gill, C. (2014). The Evolving Role of the Ombudsman: A Conceptual and Constitutional Analysis of the "Scottish Solution" to Administrative Justice. *Public Law*, 662–681.

Gill, C. (2018). Re-imagining Public Service Complaints Systems. Retrieved November 8, 2019, from https://ukaji.org/2018/10/03/re-imagining-public-sector-complaint-systems/.

Gill, C, Mullen, T, Vivian, N. (2020). The Managerial Ombudsman. *Modern Law Review* (early view), Available at: http://dx.doi.org/10.1111/1468-2230.12523.

Hertogh, M. (2001). Coercion, Cooperation, and Control: Understanding the Policy Impact of Administrative Courts and the Ombudsman in the Netherlands. *Law & Policy, 23*(1), 47–67.

Morse, Sir Amyas, Comptroller and Auditor General. (2015). Public Service Markets: Putting Things Right When They Go Wrong. Retrieved November 7, 2019, from https://www.nao.org.uk/press-release/public-service-markets-putting-things-right-when-they-go-wrong-3/.

Mullen, T., Gill, C., & Vivian, N. (2017). *Scotland's Model Complaint Handling Procedures: Exploring Recent Developments and the Usefulness of Complaint Data for Administrative Justice Research*. Project Report. University of Glasgow, Glasgow.

NAO (National Audit Office). (2015). *Public Service Markets: Putting Things Right When They Go Wrong*. HC 84.

PASC. (2013–2014). *More Complaints Please! and Time for a People's Ombudsman Service: Government Responses to the Committee's Twelfth and Fourteenth Reports of Session 2013–14*, HC 618.

PASC (Public Administration Select Committee). (2008). *When Citizens Complain*. (2007–2008) HC 409.

PHSO. 2018. *Our Strategy 2018–2021*. Retrieved November 7, 2019, from https://www.ombudsman.org.uk/sites/default/files/page/Our%20strategy%202018-2021.pdf.

PHSO (Parliamentary and Health Services Ombudsman). (2011). *Review of Government Complaint Handling 2011*. HC 799.

Simmons, R., & Brennan, C. (2017). User Voice and Complaints as Drivers of Innovation in Public Services. *Public Management Review*, *19*(8), 1085–1104.

Sinclair, D. (2008). *Fit-for-Purpose Complaint System Action Group Final Report*. Edinburgh: Scottish Government.

SPSO. (2009–2010). *Annual Report 2009–2010*. Edinburgh: SPSO.

SPSO. (2018). *Strategic Plan 2018–2020: Putting People at the Heart of Public Services*. Edinburgh: SPSO.

WHICH. (2015). *Make Complaints Count*. Retrieved November 7, 2019, from https://www.staticwhich.co.uk/documents/pdf/make-complaints-count-report%2D%2D-march-2015-397971.pdf.

CHAPTER 7

Managing Complaints: Focusing on Users and Non-users of the System

Naomi Creutzfeldt

Abstract This chapter is about the citizen's voice in an ombud process. A reformed Public Services Ombud needs to have mechanisms in place to integrate users' views into the decision-making process. This will benefit citizen's experience of the complaint process and foster legitimacy and trust in the ombud institution. Taking users' views into account in the design and management of ombuds will also help educate the public about an ombud's responsibilities and assist in getting the best out of the system. Informed by empirical evidence, the chapter focuses on three topics: (1) procedural fairness, (2) managing expectations and (3) systemic learning, data collection and reporting. I conclude with practical recommendations for an amended ombud bill, which better integrates user-views.

Keywords Ombud • User voice • Procedural fairness • Managing expectations • Systemic learning

I use the term ombud instead of ombudsman throughout this chapter.

N. Creutzfeldt (✉)
University of Westminster, London, UK
e-mail: N.Creutzfeldt@westminster.ac.uk

R. Kirkham, C. Gill (eds.), *A Manifesto for Ombudsman Reform*,
https://doi.org/10.1007/978-3-030-40612-7_7

Introduction

The introductory comments to the draft Public Service Ombudsman Bill 2016 (Cabinet Office 2016) by the then Cabinet Minister, Chris Skidmore, include reference to '[t]he core role of the Ombudsman … [as being] the investigation of complaints where a public body has not acted properly or fairly or has provided a poor service'. He also makes the claim that the Bill will 'ensure every citizen knows their voice matters and bring the Ombudsman framework into the 21st century'. Drawing on empirical evidence from a recent research project into the trust and legitimacy of ombud (Creutzfeldt 2017), in this chapter I discuss the importance of building a more user-centred approach into the ombud model and taking into account an individual's complaint journey. This journey starts with the experience of a grievance and continues on a, usually prolonged, journey to the Public Services Ombudsman (PSO). Once a complaint reaches a PSO a lot of emotional cost and time has been invested. A great responsibility is put on the ombud process to put things right, not only for the individual but also for the wider public (e.g. Kirkham 2005). Here lie challenges for process design: first, to ensure the person reaching the PSO is treated in the right way (especially at first contact); and second, to capture user data to create the opportunity for systemic learning and continued service improvement. To draw out these themes, I will focus on three topics: procedural justice, managing expectations and systemic learning. The latter goal of systemic learning involves putting systems in place that facilitate the exchange of best practice, data capture and listening to the communities ombuds serve.

As Rob Behrens, the current Parliamentary and Health Service Ombudsman (PHSO), states: 'it [the PHSO] is being transformed so that it becomes a more outward-facing, transparent organization, closer to the communities it serves, without surrendering an iota of its independence. A key challenge is to restore user and stakeholder trust and this will not be easy' (Behrens 2018: 475). A similar project is already underway at the Local Government and Social Care Ombudsman (LGSCO). In the last section I explore how this transformational goal can be built into the new PSO through legislative reform.

Procedural Fairness

In an ideal world legislative reform will create a PSO process that provides a service to the user that is fair and reasonable. The argument made here is that, in user-satisfaction terms, better outcomes will be delivered if from the beginning the user is incorporated in shaping the process. If we understand more about what users want and expect from the ombud process then we are much better placed to decide which changes need to be implemented to ensure a smoother (and fairer) process.

In multiple different scenarios, it has been empirically demonstrated, that if people experience an institution as legitimate, then they are more inclined to feel an obligation towards it and a responsibility to cooperate with it. Users are also more likely to accept decisions, not least because these are experienced as 'right and proper' when handed down by a legitimate authority (Tyler and Rasinski 1991; Gibson et al. 2003). Procedural justice research has sought to refine the relationship of procedural fairness to legitimacy and the various outcomes of trust, satisfaction, compliance and cooperation (Creutzfeldt 2018).

My empirical research has applied procedural justice theory to ombuds. This research has found that users of a PSO experience a procedure as fair and are therefore more likely to accept the outcome, if they feel: heard (*voice*); someone who is neutral is dealing with their complaint (*impartiality*); the process is *transparent*; and the process is *fair* (Tyler 2006). In particular, the data in my study showed a strong association between the perceived procedural fairness of ombud staff (mainly at first contact) and the perceived procedural fairness of the service as a whole (Creutzfeldt and Bradford 2016). The conclusion is that if a user of the ombud feels that he/she has the chance to voice his/her story and is being heard by someone who can actually do something to help and feels part of the process and that the process is impartial, then this person will more readily accept the outcome. This is the case even if the outcome is not in their favour. This is an interesting finding empirically, yet quite logical if we think about the individual who approaches an ombud (see next section).

How can this finding be more consistently translated into practice? Fulfilling these procedural justice criteria would assist a user on her/his complaint journey to experience a fair procedure. To get there we need to rethink the approach to users and help make their experience a good and fair one. A complaints process can be difficult and sometimes lengthy, yet with an understanding and appreciation of the users' perceptions of fairness this process can be significantly enhanced. This might mean investing more time early on in the process and better trained staff dealing with the complainant at the beginning of a complaint journey. Of course, such goals have to be balanced with what is possible (and affordable) in practice. However, the potential gains in user-satisfaction and long-term benefits outweigh the short-term investment.

Vulnerable Users and Non-users

The demographic that reaches ombuds most frequently is narrow and middle class (Creutzfeldt 2016), which suggests that there are limitations for the 'users' accessing ombuds (Brennan et al. 2017). This leaves a large *invisible* demographic that do not reach the ombuds. On top of this, special attention has to be paid to vulnerable users of the ombud system (ESRC Just Energy Project 2019). These are people who need even more of the above-mentioned procedural justice processes to be implemented and *felt* to be done (Brennan et al. 2017), if ombuds are to be perceived as fair. This includes more time spent on a case, ideally with the same case handler accompanying the individual through the entire process, and extra attention at the start of the interaction with the ombud process.

Again there are down-sides to this added attention. The ombud process is mainly conducted through an online medium of communication. There is the option to have a phone conversation and possibly to appear in person to discuss a case, but this involves more time, staff and cost. Nevertheless, if we are to take care of vulnerable users seriously, a few adjustments need to be made to the process. The construction of a process that works for vulnerable users—in parallel to 'business as usual'—needs careful consideration. First of all, it is important to look at what is in place already and what works. How can the existing approach best translate into a PSO? The existing experience from both PHSO and LGSCO needs to be harnessed to create a new system that vulnerable users can access more confidently. Further, careful consideration needs to be given to what this will mean for the office structure, staffing and budget. Part of this new approach can include specialised staff training and development.[1] Further, more effort needs to be put into collating best practice and creating career pathways as a caseworker/ombud with a clear career trajectory. This might

[1] The ombuds have training in place and this could be updated and ideally streamlined, at least in the form of shared learning modules, see LGSCO (2019a) and PHSO (2019a).

well be a valuable project for the Ombudsman Association to coordinate and for the PSO to be scrutinised on.

Managing Expectations

The Importance of First Contact

The argument presented here is that an important part of delivering procedural fairness is through strategies of expectations management built into systems design. Managing these expectations involves first recognising that every individual that approaches an ombud (through various existing pathways) will have already gone through an internal complaints procedure with the body they are experiencing problems with. This means that before the pathway to an ombud is open, a complainant will have experienced not only a grievance but also a failed effort at resolving the grievance. Time, energy and emotional investment already spent, the complaint origin and evolution all have to be revisited by the complainant in the ombud process. This can be a challenging experience and makes it all the more important that the first encounter with an ombud is a good one. My research has shown that the first contact can influence the overall experience and perception of a complaints process (Creutzfeldt and Bradford 2016; Creutzfeldt 2018). The first contact can set the tone for the remainder of the interaction. At this point features of the process need to be explained properly and in the remainder of the process they need to be acted upon. As outlined in Table 7.1, after the first contact, regular communication is required to maintain the management of expectations.

A preliminary issue here is that the expectations of a user—to be listened to, to be taken seriously, to speak with someone who has authority to deal with their case (Creutzfeldt 2016)—appear to run contrary to the

Table 7.1 Responsibilities during a complaints process

Manage expectations: tell the complainant what he/she can expect (responsibilities, duration, types of cases dealt with and which not, possible remedies);
Guide the complainant: active listening, continued support and clear communication are essential;
Regular update: the complainant needs to be regularly updated, even if the case is still in progress, to remind them that they are important and not being forgotten;
Provide an outcome: there needs to be an end-point of the process that is explained clearly.

budgetary restraints on ombuds for frontline staff and the *need for speed* of decision-making. Here something has to give. Empirical evidence shows that people will be more satisfied with the process if more time and human engagement is perceived to happen (Creutzfeldt 2018). High-quality interaction tends to build longer term trust in the institution and decision-acceptance. It will also help educate people about their rights and help them better understand available pathways to redress.

How does an ombud balance these competing demands? One option would be to implement a set of performance standards to be accountable to on a regular basis. This form of quality control could be externally monitored and published as part of the annual review, a point returned to later.

As a minimum, the PSO should commit to published goals of procedural fairness which explains clearly what complainants can expect. For instance, the LGSCO are guided by three principles in their complaints process. First, to provide a *transparent* process for both parties. Second, the parties are communicated with in *parity*, and third, if the local authorities want to put it right in an early resolution then it needs to happen in a *fair and just* way. This formal process is followed to make sure to be seen by the public not to have a culture of informality, or favours being called in from the local authorities.[2] In the words of Mick King, the LGSCO:

> I am critical of the culture of early settlement. The relationship that we have built with local authorities is formal, impartial, robust and professional: we are being seen to do the right thing. Local authorities might think this is unhelpful but it is important to show that there is no back channel and no special relationship. (Mick King, Interview with the author, xx, 2019)

When Things Go Wrong

Every individual experiences a complaints process differently. This means that there is no single ideal process from the users' point of view. What we can draw from this is the importance of voice in the process: giving a voice to all parties affected, it reaffirms the moral and ethical aspect of the state and its institutions—it affirms the individual's relationship with the state

[2] This approach was adopted in an attempt to avoid a common perception ten years ago, when there was criticism from the public and ombuds watchers about an informal culture of settlement between the ombuds and the local authorities.

not only on a rational level but also on a social and emotional level (Gilad 2008). This approach needs to be reliably applied and reinforced through all parts of a system to have an impact on users (Creutzfeldt 2016), especially when they experience frustration. On the back of this observation, one of the things an ombud can do is to produce a set of guidelines that form a clear and easy pathway to navigate the complaints procedure (CA 2016). Getting this right can feed directly into consumer expectations. These expectations are usually about the outcomes users desire, which means that some will inevitably remain dissatisfied.

Expectations need to be managed even more carefully when things go wrong in the decision-making process. There are several reasons why a complainant can feel dissatisfied with the way the complaint was handled and the outcome they received. Some of these reasons include: not getting the outcome they hoped for and felt entitled to; a lack of closure and a feeling of not being heard or taken seriously; the notion that they are complaining also to improve the system for others and that their effort was in vain. If a standard of service is not being met by an ombud, mechanisms need to be in place to redress this, including processes of internal review or appeal (see Chap. 7), as has become a feature in both the LGSCO (2019b) and the PHSO (2019b).

Protecting Ombud Staff: Dissatisfied Users

Managing the expectations of users is a two-way task. Although the main focus is rightly on the individual user, the sector has amongst its disgruntled complainants attracted groups of organised critics (Gill and Creutzfeldt 2018). Ombud watchers, groups of dissatisfied users of PSO schemes, engage in legal protest (Hertogh 2011) against current systems of redress for citizen-state complaints. They 'look for a voice outside of these systems and find in the internet an empowering space which allows them to reconstruct their understandings of justice in defiance of the state authority they reject' (Gill and Creutzfeldt 2018: 385, fn.11). The existence of such voices is problematic on many levels. For the sake of this chapter, I will just consider the impact persistent complainants have on case-handlers and ombuds.

Within all administrative decision-making processes there is a challenge to match user expectations with deliverables. Given the potential for tension this creates, within the design of the ombud process, the case-handlers that deal with the complainants need to be thought about and, occasionally, protected (Gill et al. 2017; PHSO 2019c). Case workers, complaint handlers and ombuds need to get the balance right between managing the divide between users' expectations and the actual experience.

People usually are not sure what to expect from an ombud process and tend to have expectations that are too high. As noted above, special attention has to be given to manage user expectations from the outset. Here lies the opportunity and challenge to set the tone for the rest of the engagement in the process. The tone in which a decision is delivered to the complainant makes a difference. The way in which a decision is communicated will affect how a complainant responds to, understands and accepts the outcome. Decision-making also has to be delivered in a language that is easily accessible and transparent for the complainant. As Behrens (2018) suggests, 'the user needs to be reminded that while the complaint is their own, the investigation and adjudications are the ombudsman's within clear and accessible policy frameworks' (ibid.: 463). Ombuds argue that there always will be disgruntled people and that they would not 'go away' if there were *fairer* processes. This tension reveals the core of the problem—better communication and a perceived fairer process are necessary to address these deep-rooted concerns. The discussion about managing expectations piggy-backs on a long agenda in public administration of encouraging service providers to take users more seriously (e.g. Cabinet Office 1991; PASC 2014). A continued effort to make the ombud process easier to understand and to experience for the user is necessary to build trust in the process and help address underlying concerns as well as foster a better relationship.

Data Collection, Reporting and Systemic Learning

Transparency and Procedural Fairness

Procedural fairness goes beyond the handling of individual complaints and also entails building trust in the office through being transparent about, and reporting on, performance (see Chap. 7). This goal requires the collation of data. The draft Bill offers only a brief list of requirements in this regard (Cabinet Office 2016: Sched. 1, cls. 6 and 7), but one model to draw ideas from is the private sector, in which ombuds have had to adjust their services according to the EU-wide Consumer ADR Directive (2013/11/EU) that sets minimum standards (Cortés 2016; Briard 2019). This new framework aimed to create improvements in the procedural design of alternative dispute resolution (ADR) bodies, to enhance legitimacy and to create a standard of annual reporting and data collection (more below). The value and effectiveness of the ADR Directive has been disputed, with some concerned that the data collected is driven more by what is easy to gather than a drive for transparency. Nor is it clear that much attention is given to analysing the results. However, the importance of collecting user data lies in its potential for long-term learning, understanding users' behavioural patterns and detecting trends. These goals translate directly into the public sector, and establishing a degree of standardisation and consistency in the performance standards reported on would aid transparency and understanding.

Using Data to Deliver Systemic Learning

Similar concerns can be raised with the desire to collect complaint-handling data for the purpose of detecting trends and identifying systemic issues before they might escalate. Ideally, such a capacity to look at the wider data allows a PSO to understand what can be done differently not to cause repeat problems. Being able to observe how complaints have generated change might assist users in understanding the procedural fairness of a PSO.

Some of this work already occurs. For instance, the LGSCO publishes systemic and thematic reports to feedback learning to public authorities and local care providers. These are usually accompanied by a media release. The LGSCO also publishes hands-on technical advice notes for the sector and have developed a training programme, with its own complaint handlers delivering the training.

However, there are no streamlined methods in the wider complaints sector for collecting user data at the moment. Different ombuds adopt different approaches to data collection and work with different case management systems. This problem multiplies when trying to integrate data from local complaint-handling schemes. If there was a common method to collect data (and to report it) then this would be immensely valuable. This data could then be shared with other bodies (e.g. other ombuds, local authorities, the NHS) to help improve the dispute resolution and decision-making process. The moment of legislative PSO reform could be a great opportunity to invest in a refreshed approach (Frank 2000). With new powers (see Chaps. 4 and 5), the new PSO could produce (shared) guidelines about which data to collect and be clear about why it matters.

This could be part of the Complaints Standard Authority function (see Chap. 5) and needs to be a fluid process, regularly revisited in consultation with stakeholders to be able to react to identified trends or to pay more attention to potential areas of concern. If one were to find a way in which to collect data in a systematic manner, many possibilities of comparisons, identifying best practice and a continued exchange of experiences could become apparent (Hodges 2016).

Using Learning to Advance Complaint-Handling

There are some examples of PSO already making use of learning from complaints and reporting and interacting closely with public bodies. The PHSO's current strategic plan (PHSO 2018–2021) incorporates both the improvement of interaction with complainants during the complaints process and developing relationships with bodies in jurisdiction to improve frontline complaint-handling. Initial contact is handled by a dedicated Intake team, all of whom have undertaken a professional skills training programme which includes modules on scoping and risk management, as well as investigative and communication skills. All case-handlers also benefit from dedicated training in vicarious trauma and equality, diversity and inclusion. To facilitate user engagement, processes for early resolution and mediation now stand alongside traditional adjudication. Further:

> an independent, external research company undertakes telephone interviews with around 600 complainants each quarter to get feedback from complainants at various stages in our process, and to ascertain the extent to which commitments in PHSO's Service Charter are being met. (Rob Behrens, PHSO Ombudsman, Interview with the author, 2019)[3]

In line with the third strand of its *Strategic Plan* PHSO is now actively engaged in developing and consulting on a Good Practice Complaints Framework for all bodies in jurisdiction. This initiative has been warmly welcomed as much needed in NHS Trusts, and is endorsed by health service regulators and complainant groups as a key contribution to improving service delivery. With the framework comes the potential of a nationally recognised complaints standards and PHSO-sponsored training for complaints handlers. As current PHSO Ombudsman, Rob Behrens, made clear:

[3] Returns are published each quarter (https://www.ombudsman.org.uk/service-charter)

> We cannot sit around waiting for Government and Parliament to deliver the long-promised statutory reform of ombudsman services as if we were 'Waiting for Godot'. Successful statutory reform rarely comes from a blank piece of paper but needs to incorporate something of contemporary good practice and practice endorsed by both independent peer review and parliamentary oversight. (ibid.)[4]

To conclude, the new PSO needs to have a plan about how to include voices of its users into the design of the process. This is not a static one-off choice, but rather needs to be a conscious and proactive ongoing effort. This approach will not only benefit the user of the PSO and the staff dealing with individual complaints but also produce longer term trust and legitimacy of the ombud institution.

Practical Considerations for the Design of a Public Services Ombudsman

General Duties and Specific Requirements

Building on the topics discussed, I suggest to include three general duties in the PSO Bill (and the design of the PSO process) backed up by specific publishing requirements to ensure an accountability system is in place to implement good practice.

1. Giving complainants a voice in the process translates into a *duty to be procedurally fair.*
2. Managing expectations translates into a *duty of care towards complainants.*
3. Collecting data translates into *a duty to learning from and integrating users' views into the decision-making process.*

By themselves the general duties would have no real bite, but would emphasise the importance of the matters identified in this chapter and frame subsequent scrutiny of the PSO's performance. In this latter respect, the specific publishing requirements on the PSO would identify obligations that the PSO would have to evidence before the PSO Board (as well

[4] See also (Tyndall et al. 2018: 7; PACAC 2019).

as publicly) and would be targeted at evidencing how the duties were being delivered. For instance:

- The PSO should have a duty to provide *guidance* on the standards it applies in delivering its duties towards complainants;
- There needs to be an obligation to *report* on how the PSO deliver its duties;
- The PSO should report on a programme for *staff training* that evolves; and
- A *regular (external) review* needs to be in place.

Details of the Guidance That Would Need to Be Reported on

This approach towards requiring the PSO to evidence its approach and performance would represent a big step forward on the current formal arrangements. Although the current draft Bill provides for some reporting duties on performance (Cabinet Office 2016: Sched. 2), it is limited, requiring only the provision of:

> information about—(a) how long investigations that were completed in the financial year in question took to be completed, (b) how many of those investigations took more than 12 months to be completed, and (c) the action being taken with a view to securing that all investigations are completed within 12 months. (ibid.: para. 21(3))

As noted above, this obligation does not go as far as the Consumer ADR Directive 2013/11/EU which details a series of additional data requirements that could be integrated into a new ombuds Bill (Creutzfeldt 2016; Kirkham 2016). The current draft Bill does establish a Board to oversee the PSO (para. 23 (1)), stating:

> The Board must monitor the carrying out of the Ombudsman's functions under this Act, with particular reference to the quality and efficiency of the service provided by the Ombudsman and the desirability of securing improvements in that service. (ibid.)

But here too, the Consumer ADR Directive goes further:

> In order to ensure that ADR entities function properly and effectively, they should be closely monitored. [...] [C]ompetent authorities should publish regular reports on the development and functioning of ADR entities in their Member States. [...]. (Article 55)

The Consumer ADR Directive aimed to promote high-quality alternative dispute resolution (ADR) for consumers. This included a commitment to continued monitoring of ADR providers and to a set of benchmarks that map onto the procedural fairness demands alluded to in this chapter, such as: impartiality, independence, expertise (art 6), transparency (art 7), accessibility, fairness (art 9), timeliness and effectiveness (art 8) of their procedures (box 2). The PSO could be required to report on all of these standards. A similar expectation could be made about the criteria for decision-making, namely maladministration, injustice and service failure, and the PSO's more detailed understanding as to how those principles should apply in practice. The public confidence in decisions will depend in part on how well these accounts and definitions are accepted upon review.

A further example of guidance that the PSO should be required to provide can be found in the Jersey Law Commission report. It spells out a duty of the PSO to communicate and educate about its role:

> The detail of the outreach and communications activities would not need to be specified in the legislation establishing the Ombudsman, but the Jersey Law Commission recommends that the Public Services (Ombudsman) Jersey Law should contain a broad duty on the Ombudsman to undertake activities to inform people and public bodies within its remit about its role. (Jersey Law Commission 2018: 63)

The Importance and Reach of the Reporting Duty

The examples above illustrate a range of publishing duties on the PSO that would enable the Board and/or Parliament to hold the office accountable for performance. In many instances, as a result of good practice in the sector, existing PSO already provide detail and base their performance reporting on these, or similar, criteria. Nevertheless, it is strongly advised that this best practice is now detailed as a requirement in legislation.

Importantly, accountability should be seen as a concept that goes further than the Board and Parliament. Here is where an element of user voice also needs to be present. There needs to be an embedded process through which users input into the decision-making process. A new bill could therefore include a commitment to regular:

- consultations with users and case-handlers;
- feedback from users and case-handlers;
- focus groups and surveys;
- reporting annually on success on these duties;
- providing guidance on how these duties are delivered towards complainants; and
- there needs to be a policy how to deal with people who continue to complain (e.g. see Scottish Public Services Ombudsman 2019).

Ideally these suggested practices could be adopted (and agreed upon) by other bodies to allow for regular and streamlined data collection. This would allow for a baseline to be established and to explore what best practice looks like. Regular checks on quality of decision-making, training needed and how complaints processes are developing would be part of the new PSO framework. The Ombudsman Association *Service Standards Framework* (OA 2017) can play an important role in bringing PSO together and working towards a shared approach. The framework provides measures on five commitments to service users (similar to the ADR Directive) on accessibility; communication; professionalism; fairness and transparency.

In a wider approach, PSO could commit to shared standards which might look like those produced by the ANZOA (an ombudsman association group for Australasian schemes), which has six guiding principles (accessibility, independence, fairness, accountability, efficiency and effectiveness) and also a series of evaluation standards:

- Complaint numbers and statistics;
- Complaint efficiency and costing;
- Budget reporting; cost benefit analysis;
- Staff statistical analysis and staffing changes;
- Customer satisfaction surveys;
- Comparative complaints analysis;
- Benchmarking against a strategic plan or value statement
- Benchmarking against other offices;
- Case studies;
- Office observation (on its own performance);

- Unsolicited feedback;
- comments on performance of agencies;
- outreach activities;
- speeches;
- training;
- policy changes; publicity; identifying complaints about ombuds themselves and how an office is held to account. (Stuhmke 2018)

To conclude, there is a huge opportunity to invigorate the ombud procedure and standing in the community. Paths suggested in this chapter are: to be aware of the user journey; incorporating users' voice into the process design; and learning from collected data of past and current users to improve the system. Bold new duties and strong leadership are a good combination to bring about change. The PSO needs to build on what works well at present and remodel crumbling structures (see O'Brien 2015). Users need to be involved in this process and become part of an ongoing scrutiny to establish a system that works and that is perceived to be fair.

References

Behrens, R. (2018). Ombudsman Values – A Guide to Practise. In M. Hertogh & R. Kirkham (Eds.), *Research Handbook on the Ombudsman*. Cheltenham: Edward Elgar.

Brennan, C., Sourdin, T., Williams, J., Burstyner, N., & Gill, C. (2017). Consumer Vulnerability and Complaint Handling: Challenges, Opportunities and Dispute System Design. *International Journal of Consumer Studies, 41*(6), 638–646.

Briard, A. (2019). Impact of Directive 2013/11/EU on Consumer ADR Quality: Evidence from France and the UK. *Journal of Consumer Policy, 42*(1), 109–147.

Cabinet Office. (1991). *The Citizen's Charter: Raising the Standard*. Cm. 1599.

Cabinet Office. (2016). *Draft Public Service Ombudsman Bill*. Cm. 9374.

Citizens Advice. (2016). *Understanding Consumer Experiences of Complaint Handling*. Retrieved October 31, 2019, from https://www.citizensadvice.org.uk/Global/CitizensAdvice/Consumer%20publications/Understanding%20consumer%20experiences%20of%20complaint%20handling_DJS%20report%20final_June2016%20(2)%20(1).pdf.

Cortés, P. (Ed.). (2016). *The New Regulatory Framework for Consumer Dispute Resolution*. Oxford: Oxford University Press.

Creutzfeldt, N. (2016). A Voice for Change? The Trust Relationships Between Ombudsmen, Individuals and Public Service Providers. *Journal of Social Welfare and Family Law, 38*(4), 460–479.

Creutzfeldt, N. (2017). Trusting the Middle Man: Impact and Legitimacy of Ombudsmen in Europe. Retrieved October 31, 2019, from https://www.law.ox.ac.uk/trusting-middle-man-impact-and-legitimacy-ombudsmen-europe.

Creutzfeldt, N. (2018). *Ombudsmen and ADR: A Comparative Study of Informal Justice in Europe*. London: Palgrave Macmillan.

Creutzfeldt, N., & Bradford, B. (2016). Dispute Resolution Outside of Courts: Procedural Justice and Decision Acceptance Among Users of Ombuds Services in the UK. *Law and Society Review, 50*(4), 985–1016.

ESRC Just Energy Project. (2019). Retrieved October 31, 2019, from https://esrcjustenergy.wordpress.com.

Frank, B. (2000). *Ombudsman Best Practices: Supporting Culture Change to Promote Individualized Care in Nursing Homes*. Retrieved October 31, 2019, from https://ltcombudsman.org/uploads/files/issues/Best-Practices-Paper-Ombudsman-Culture-Change.pdf.

Gibson, J. L., Caldeira, G. A., & Spence, L. K. (2003). Measuring Attitudes Toward the United States Supreme Court. *American Journal of Political Science, 47*, 354–367.

Gilad, S. (2008). Accountability or Expectations Management? The Role of the Ombudsman in Financial Regulation. *Law and Policy, 30*(2), 227–253.

Gill, C., & Creutzfeldt, N. (2018). The 'Ombuds Watchers': Dissatisfaction, Collective Dissent, and Legal Protest Amongst Users of Public Service Ombuds. *Social & Legal Studies, 27*(3), 367–388.

Gill, C., Hirst, C., Sapouna, M., & Williams, J. (2017). *How Do Complaints Affect Those Complained About? An Empirical Investigation into the Effects of Complaints on Public Service Employees*. Retrieved October 31, 2019, from https://esrcjustenergy.files.wordpress.com/2018/01/how-do-complaints-affect-those-complained-about.pdf.

Hertogh, M. (2011). Loyalists, Legalists, Cynics and Outsiders: Who Are the Critics of the Justice System in the UK and the Netherlands? *International Journal of Law in Context, 7*(1), 31–46.

Hodges, C. (2016). Consumer Redress: Implementing the Vision. In P. Cortés (Ed.), *The New Regulatory Framework for Consumer Dispute Resolution*. Oxford: Oxford University Press.

Jersey Law Commission. (2018). Designing a Public Services Ombudsman for Jersey. Retrieved November 4, 2019, from https://jerseylawcommission.files.wordpress.com/2018/11/jsylawcom_designingombudsman_final.pdf.

Kirkham, R. (2005). A Complainant's View of the Local Government Ombudsman. *Journal of Social Welfare and Family Law, 27*(3–4), 383–394.

Kirkham, R. (2016). Regulating ADR: Lessons from the UK. In P. Cortes (Ed.), *The Transformation of Consumer Dispute Resolution in the European Union: A Renewed Approach to Consumer Protection*. Oxford: Oxford University Press.

LGSCO. (2019a). Retrieved October 31, 2019, from https://www.lgo.org.uk/training.

LGSCO. (2019b). *Complaints About Our Service*. Retrieved October 31, 2019, from https://www.lgo.org.uk/information-centre/about-us/our-performance/complaints-about-our-service.

O'Brien, N. (2015). What Future for the Ombudsman? *The Political Quarterly, 86*(1), 907–924.

Ombudsman Association. (2017). *Service Standards Framework*. Retrieved October 31, 2019, from https://www.ombudsmanassociation.org/docs/OA17_Service_Standards_2017_Final.pdf.

PASC. (2014). *More Complaints Please!* HC 229.

PHSO. (2018–2021). *Our Strategy 2018–21*. Retrieved October 31, 2019, from https://www.ombudsman.org.uk/about-us/corporate-information/corporate-publications.

PHSO. (2019a). Retrieved October 31, 2019, from https://www.ombudsman.org.uk/news-and-blog/blog/working-partnership-improve-complaint-handling.

PHSO. (2019b). *Feedback About Our Service*. Retrieved October 31, 2019, from https://www.ombudsman.org.uk/about-us/feedback-about-our-service.

PHSO. (2019c). *Service Model Policy and Guidance: General Guidance*. Retrieved October 31, 2019, from https://www.ombudsman.org.uk/sites/default/files/Service%20Model_general_guidance_23_8_2018_0.pdf.

Public Administration and Constitutional Affairs Committee 'Independent Review of the Financial Ombudsman Service' 2019 available at: https://www.parliament.uk/business/committees/committees-a-z/commons-select/treasury-committee/inquiries1/parliament-2017/independent-review-financial-ombudsman-service-17-19/

Scottish Public Services Ombudsman. (2019). *Unacceptable Actions Policy*. Retrieved October 31, 2019, from https://www.spso.org.uk/sites/spso/files/communications_material/leaflets_public/general/Unacceptable%20Actions%20Policy.pdf.

Stuhmke, A. (2018). 'Ombuds Can, Ombuds Can't, Ombuds Should, Ombuds Shan't: A Call to Improve Evaluation of the Ombudsman Institution. In M. Hertogh & R. Kirkham (Eds.), *Research Handbook on the Ombudsman*. London: Edward Elgar Publishing.

Tyler, T. (2006). *Why People Obey the Law*. Princeton: Princeton University Press.

Tyler, T., & Rasinski, K. (1991). Procedural Justice, Institutional Legitimacy, and the Acceptance of Unpopular U.S. Supreme Court Decisions: A Reply to Gibson. *Law & Society Review, 25*(3), 621–630.

Tyndall, P., Mitchell C., & Gill, C. (2018). *Value for Money Study: Report of the Independent Peer Review of the Parliamentary and Health Service Ombudsman*. Retrieved November 8, 2019, from https://www.ombudsman.org.uk/sites/default/files/Value_for_Money_report_final.pdf.

CHAPTER 8

Strengthening Procedural Fairness and Transparency Through Ombudsman Legislation

Richard Kirkham

Abstract This chapter explores a range of legislative reform measures that will add clarity and refinement to the powers and procedural fairness of the ombud design. Some are relatively minor and uncontentious, while others address flaws that have been identified in legal dispute. Not all were included in the 2016 draft Bill. This chapter also highlights how, as pressure on it has grown, the ombud sector has taken the initiative in devising new techniques to allow for enhanced accountability. These include measures to be more transparent in decision-making and to reconsider its decisions, and these new practices should now be made a duty in legislation. Finally, the chapter argues for the new legislation to be written in framework form wherever possible, to facilitate subsequent flexibility and amendment.

Keywords Procedural fairness • Accountability • Transparency • Legislative design • Legislative reform

R. Kirkham (✉)
Sheffield University, Sheffield, UK
e-mail: r.m.kirkham@sheffield.ac.uk

R. Kirkham, C. Gill (eds.), *A Manifesto for Ombudsman Reform*,
https://doi.org/10.1007/978-3-030-40612-7_8

Introduction

Much of the discussion on ombud reform revolves around making the office more effective by broadening its powers. However, the other main challenge for the office, as highlighted in the previous chapter, is to manage its relations with complainants and retain its reputation for delivering quality justice. Perceptions of, and trust in (Creutzfeldt 2016), the ombud's decision-making processes has varied and organised user voices have publicly critiqued the sector (Gill and Creutzfeldt 2018). The standard public law response to this challenge is to build in safeguards that guarantee appropriate levels of procedural fairness and accountability.

In exploring this issue, this chapter details those areas in existing legislation that place insufficient emphasis on the ombud's powers and decision-making standards. The sources of ideas for this reform agenda come from the interventions of the courts and legislative precedents elsewhere. But additionally, the pursuit of reputational legitimacy has led to the ombud sector itself innovating to make the office more accountable for its actions and performance, and to enhance procedural fairness. The chapter argues that there would be benefits in institutionalising in legislation some of these developments. However, it will also be argued that care should be taken not to over-legislate. A preferable model for ombud legislation is one of establishing a framework of duties on the office, the detail of which is then left to be resolved and updated on a rolling basis through an ongoing dialogue between the new Public Sector Ombudsman (PSO) and those charged with overseeing the scheme.

The Importance of Ombudsman Accountability

The unwritten working assumption which underpins the ombud model is the importance of delivering justice. Insofar as this task involves complaint-handling, it is organised through a public policy trade-off, with ombuds operating in a lighter-touch regulatory environment when compared to the heavily rationed provision of formal justice in the courts. Hence for ombuds, there is no specific qualification route into the profession, no opportunity for adversarial representation, no capacity to appeal,[1] no

[1] Formally, there are two exceptions to this in the SLCC and the Pensions Ombudsman, but by law both are heavily circumscribed appeal routes, see Legal Profession and Legal Aid (Scotland) Act 2007: s.21 and Pension Schemes Act 1993: s. 151(4).

public hearings or full transparency of proceedings. Instead, the emphasis on ombuds is to deliver a free 'efficient and mass processing' informal form of justice through a model that uses more flexible methods of inquiry, looser grounds and a less rigid approach to procedural fairness. The motivation for this trade-off in favour of encouraging ombud dispute resolution has largely been a pragmatic one: namely, the need to respond to citizen demand for the redress of grievances and the lack of capacity to deliver justice through the judicial system alone (Koo 2018). These underlying drivers continue to dominate public policy discourse (e.g. Bach Commission 2017; Civil Justice Council 2018) and look set to continue. There are, however, 'rule of law' and 'practical' risks in underplaying the nature of the ombud's role and downgrading the importance of the standards that apply in the sector.

On the rule of law side, there are a series of long-standing concerns with the growth of all forms of alternative dispute resolution (ADR). Some relate to the potential for ADR to encourage negotiated settlements disadvantageous to the weaker party. Others to the absence of judicial consideration and precedent over large areas of civil justice that might result from overuse of ADR (Fiss 1984; Genn 2012). A broader concern is the loss of a sense of the intrinsic public value of justice systems if too much onus is placed on 'the consumerization of civil justice' (Neuberger 2010: para. 14).

On the practical side, not only are we reliant upon the ombud sector to resolve large numbers of disputes, many grievances pursued with an ombud tackle issues of considerable financial value, emotional and physical content. Many impact profoundly on individual careers and professional integrity. Even grievances that appear to the external observer to have low import will have deep-rooted significance for the individual in their experience of dealing with public and private institutional power. Overall, therefore, the public, and potentially therapeutic, benefits of channelling grievances through the ombud sector are high. But to achieve these benefits, ombud processes need to be capable of delivering justice in a manner that retains public and stakeholder confidence for the long term.

In addressing these concerns, most ombud legislation is limited in the formal procedures they require to provide reassurance as to the quality of decision-making. This absence of detail stands at odds to the internal logic of the ombud model, which is to take complaints seriously and 'put things right' (e.g. PHSO 2009). The legislative under-regulation of standards also looks out of date given the lived experience of the sector, which is constantly under pressure from users to legitimate its decision-making (Gill and Creutzfeldt 2018). Parliament too has on occasion been critical of ombud performance (Communities and Local Government Committee 2012–2013).

The nature of any justice institution's work makes it unlikely that all users will feel satisfied with outcomes that go against them. Nevertheless, the sector has long since understood the need to respond to the concerns of complainants and new solutions have been devised, in part because of the intervention of the courts. These solutions will be considered here in two stages. First, those solutions which are better described as refinements and updates. Second, those solutions which have been developed in direct response to the enhanced expectations on the sector.

Implementing the Lessons of Experience

Many necessary reforms are relatively prosaic in nature but nevertheless highly important. In order to perform its core functions, the ombud requires a range of legislatively proscribed discretionary powers. Unsurprisingly, over time, flaws and ambiguities have been found in the drafting of those powers, and some aspects have become out of fit with modern practice. Occasionally, ambiguity in legislation has resulted in legal challenges to ombud decision-making and has raised issues of procedural fairness.

Through a combination of legal intervention and temporary pragmatic measures, the weaknesses in older legislation have generally proved patchable. But to avoid future confusion, many of these points of law would be best reconfirmed in legislation, and a series of major and minor corrective proposals have been put forward. The legislative alternatives across the UK and elsewhere, and the experience of their operation, provide rich pickings and comparative lessons in the art of how to do, and how not to do, ombud design.

Table 8.1 details first those proposals already included in the 2016 draft Bill, most of which should be uncontroversial as they arise merely from the flow of experience, such as allowing for direct access as well as flexibility in the process by which complaints are submitted.[2] A good example where

[2] On this matter, see Public Administration Committee 2014: para. 55. A recent experiment in recreating a similar filter for the Housing Ombudsman has been reported as only successful in a minority of cases, whilst otherwise placing a fresh block and delay mechanism

Table 8.1 Recommended legislative reform proposals to the ombudsman's discretionary powers

Clarification to ombudsman powers listed in Draft Public Services Ombudsman Bill		*Powers that should also be included and further clarified*	
Receipt of complaint (cl.14-5) Referral of complaints to the ombudsman (cl.18) Reopening and expanding investigations on the basis of new evidence (cl.4(6) and cl.13) Power to investigate private bodies (cl.6(2)) Power to adopt informal techniques (cl.10(5)) Distinction between findings and recommendations (cl.14(8))	Definition of administrative fault (cl.6(1)) Jurisdiction of ombudsman where alternative remedy might be available (cl.7)[a] Duty to give notice on establishing terms of investigation Confirmation that recommendations have been implemented	Power to make a financial recommendation Making ombudsman findings binding Power and duty to share information Ombudsman power to quash its own decision Duty to explain standards of clinical failure applied	Power to launch an own-initiative investigation Power to operate as a Complaint Standards Authority Power to refer legal question to the courts Power of Parliament (or executive) to refer matter to ombudsman[b] Power of court to stay proceedings

[a]On this legal issue, see *R v Commissioner for Local Administration ex parte Croydon LBC* [1989] 1 All ER 1033; *R v Local Commissioner For Local Government Ex p Liverpool* [2000] EWCA Civ 54

[b]For example, see Ombudsperson Act (British Columbia), s.10(3); Ombudsman Act (New Zealand), s.13(5)

adopting comparative solutions provides an easy answer is the need to clarify the processes by which it is confirmed that recommendations have been implemented, with several schemes offering models by which reporting duties can be confirmed in legislation (see, for instance, the Law Commission 2011: 51–62). However, the 2016 draft Bill has also showed innovation, as for instance in providing the PSO with powers to expand its investigation beyond a specific complaint if 'additional matters' come to the 'Ombudsman's attention'(Cabinet Office 2016: cl.13(1)).[3]

in the dispute resolution process burdening almost all parties involved (Housing Ombudsman 2018b: 8–9).

[3]This measure addresses the legal problem raised in *Cavanagh & Ors v Health Service Commissioner* [2005] EWCA Civ 1578; *Miller & Anor v The Health Service Commissioner for England* [2018] EWCA Civ 144.

Other reform proposals though pick up on lessons learnt from case law and experience elsewhere, not all of these were dealt with in the 2016 draft Bill and are separately listed in Table 8.1. Arguably, readdressing some of these points in legislation is unnecessary, given past judicial intervention. However, not only would confirming such contentious points of law in legislation bring enhanced transparency to the law, judicial intervention has left uncertain some legal questions which touch on wider 'political' concerns. Such issues include:

- The circumstances in which the PSO should be able to recommend financial compensation, particularly where an alternative remedy may have been available (*JR55* [2016] UKSC 22).
- The legal status of the PSO's findings, with the current legal rule subtly different for the LGO and the PHSO (*R v Commissioner for Local Administration ex p Eastleigh BC* [1988] QB 855; *R (Bradley) v Secretary of State for Work and Pensions and Parliamentary Commissioner for Administration* [2007] EWHC 242 (Admin)).
- The duty of the PSO to share information between parties. (*R v Local Commissioner For Local Government Ex p Turpin* [2002] JPL 326).
- The standard that needs to be applied to demonstrate clinical failure (*Atwood v The Health Service Commissioner* [2008] EWHC 2315; *Miller & Anor v The Health Service Commissioner for England* [2018] EWCA Civ 144).

Although they have not yet been subject to litigation before the courts, there are other legal questions that have arisen in ombud practice that could be usefully cleared up. For instance, does a PSO have the power to quash its own decision in circumstances where subsequently it came to light that it had made an error?[4]

Acknowledging Procedural Fairness Innovation

Innovation in the ombud sector does not just derive from legislative developments elsewhere, or through judicial decision-making. In many instances, the driver for reform is the ombud sector itself through the

[4] This became a major factor for the PHSO which has recently reversed a previous policy of not quashing reports (PACAC 2016–17: 11–12). The point in law, however, remains unclear.

development of practices that enhance the ombud model. The question then becomes whether those new practices should be confirmed in legislation. This section explores three important examples that fall into this category.

Publication of Decisions

An ombud adjudicates and makes decisions on complaints. A question that arises from this function is the extent to which it is necessary for decisions made to be published. On this issue there is considerable looseness, and it might be argued laxity, in existing law on the standards that operate in the sector. This creates space for criticism and concerns as to the integrity of the decision-making process operated. Standard criticisms concern the competence of decision-makers, an excessive reliance on paper-based decision-making, institutional bias towards service providers, the general opaque nature of decision-making and the absence of a detailed definition of the standards applied (Harlow 2018: 76–82). Such allegations are difficult to refute but, in partial response, the practice of a number of schemes is to publish online all reports and decision statements.

The move towards open publication has in large part been driven by a desire and/or need to defend and demonstrate the quality of justice an ombud provides. Publication policies provide a means to improve the institution's claim to providing justice in two specific regards: through (i) detailing the reasoning and good administration standards being applied in decision-making and (ii) providing a public defence of the quality and procedural fairness of ombudsman decision-making. Publication policies have a further value in the disciplining effect that the exercise places on ombud offices to defend their reasoning,[5] and also offer potential in terms of evidencing the consistency in which the office applies standards of administrative fault. Along these lines, the Financial Ombudsman Services (FOS) described the reasons for its publication policy as to:

- ensure that our stakeholders had access to a full, accurate and balanced picture of the decisions we reach;
- ensure that interested parties could see for themselves the decision we made …;

[5] Nb Schedule 1, para 7 of the Draft Public Services Ombudsman Bill, partly addresses this point but as currently written is insufficient.

- avoid any risk of being seen to 'editorialise' on which decisions should be publicly available; …
- set clear guidelines about what information should not be included in the decisions we publish; and
- give further assurance to our stakeholders about the quality and consistency of our work. (Financial Ombudsman Service 2011: 9)

Although all ombuds are required to provide reasons for their decisions to the parties to a dispute, currently only FOS is under a statutory duty to publish all 'determinations' (Financial Services and Markets Act 2000: s.230A(1)). The Local Government and Social Care Ombudsman already has a full publication policy for its decision-making (LGSCO 2019), and the PHSO has committed to introducing one (PHSO 2018: 14). This commitment should be converted into a statutory duty for the new PSO.

Decision and Service Review

Part of the trade-off in favour of the ombud as a justice provider has been a general acceptance that an ombud's decision should be considered as final, with no further layers of scrutiny. This choice has meant that the court's role in hearing complaint grievances has been only a supervisory one (Kirkham and Stuhmcke, forthcoming). This supervisory role, ordinarily delivered through judicial review, is one that leads to very few ombud decisions being overturned (ibid.). This is not to say that judicial review has not been influential, but it is ordinarily an unrealistic option for complainants seeking to challenge a decision.

The difficulty with this arrangement is that the absence of an additional appeal option contributes to a generic concern with ADR that it weakens the capacity of justice systems to arrive at a 'just' decision due to the more opaque and less rule-bound processes applied. Two solutions have evolved internally to address this 'justice void' that should now be confirmed in legislation.

First, providing complainants with an opportunity for a service review is now a universal feature of the ombud process, described by the Scottish Public Services Ombudsman as:

> a customer service complaint is: [a]n expression of dissatisfaction by one or more individuals (including bodies under … jurisdiction) about the [ombudsman's] action or lack of action in relation to our service or about the standard of service provided by or on behalf of the [ombudsman]. (SPSO 2018)

The need for a service review mechanism creates few debates, other than the degree to which they are effective or would benefit from an independent element tagged onto the process. By contrast, there remains more disagreement around the need for, and the role of, an additional stage which allows for the ombud decision itself to be reviewed internally.

As noted above, there is a tension in the ombud technique between the goal of bringing a complaint to a close and providing the optimum level of procedural fairness. A common line in the sector has always been that an ombud owns a complaint, and once a decision has been made proportionate dispute resolution requires finality. Under stakeholder pressure, in particular from complainants, that standard line is looking increasingly unsustainable and several schemes have now developed transparent formal processes of decision review.

The argument for a decision review process is well expressed by the Housing Ombudsman:

> *Fairness*
> There is no appeal against the Ombudsman's determinations. Our process must however be conducted in a way that is fair to the parties. This means that we must provide an opportunity to the parties to understand and challenge the basis of our determinations.
>
> *Customer care*
> People often seek review of our determinations because they do not agree with them. However, there are also those who may not understand them. A review can be used to help the parties understand our decisions. It is an opportunity to provide further explanation where the parties appear not to have understood either the determination itself, or the way in which it was made.
>
> *Risk mitigation*
> In the absence of an appeal mechanism the only route available to the parties to challenge any of our decisions is to seek judicial review. Although opportunities for the parties to seek judicial review are limited, the consequences for the Service could be serious. Reviewing a determination mitigates against the risks of both judicial review proceedings being started and being successful. (Housing Ombudsman 2018a: 1)

Being an internal process, there will be a limit to which the perception of fairness can be enhanced by decision review, but the records of those schemes that operate them show that a good number do lead to decisions being reopened (Kirkham forthcoming). In other words, even if in most reviews the original decision is upheld, the decision review process does identify errors and thereby exercises an important mode of quality control that is potentially beneficial for institutional learning within the ombud office.

In order to shore up this shift in ombud practice, the new PSO should be under a statutory duty to operate both a decision and a service review process, and be required to report on the throughput and outcomes of cases considered.

A Quality Assurance Board

Many ombuds now deploy a range of boards or forums, made up of stakeholders and relevant expertise, to offer both constructive criticism and guidance to the scheme and to identify relevant viewpoints. One idea from some private sector schemes develops this approach by establishing a 'Standards Board' to concentrate attention on the standards applied in decision-making. A Standards Board is made up of a cross-section of interested parties in the issues raised in ombudsman complaints, for example representatives of users of services, providers and regulators. Its role is not to reconsider ombud decisions but to offer feedback on a sample. For instance, the Bye-Laws Governing the Furniture Ombudsman's Standards Board state:

> The Ombudsman's Standards Board helps to provide an invaluable set of checks and balances by advising us on our rules, practices and procedures and by reviewing a cross section of our decided cases in order to provide independent feedback to our staff. This helps to ensure that our decisions continue to be fair and equitable for all parties. (Dispute Resolution Ombudsman 2018)

As with the proposals on publishing decisions and integrating decision reviews, the goal is twofold: first, to provide increased assurance that fair and correct decisions are being made and, second, to integrate a forum in which the standards being applied within an office are being challenged and tested from external perspectives. To avoid confusion with existing or former 'Standards Boards' set up to consider breaches of public standards by public officers, a new title, such as 'Quality Assurance Board', should be applied for PSO.

A Future-Proofing Strategy of Legislative Design

The design of PSO legislation has altered somewhat over the years but thought should be given as to the best approach to adopt for the proposed new scheme. The Parliamentary Commissioners Act 1967 is regularly critiqued as outdated but at 25 pages long it was commendably brief compared to more recent examples which have become ever more detailed and extensive (e.g. Public Service Ombudsman (Wales) Act 2019). A key benefit was that the 1967 Act provided the new office with much room to establish an operating model suitable to its then novel task. To achieve this flexibility, the ombud was given very broad discretionary powers and many issues now considered integral to the office were left silent. This looseness can be problematic, but it would be wise to leave space in future PSO legislation for real experience and experimentation to evolve, rather than attempting to predict all eventualities in advance.

The challenge is to provide the PSO with sufficient power whilst simultaneously establishing control arrangements that provide stakeholders with reassurance as to its future activity. In striking the right balance, a key benefit that the drafters of the new PSO possess is that there is a wide diversity of legislation to copy from, and experience to integrate. Along with past experience, guidance on designing dispute resolution processes can be found in several sources (e.g. Bondy and Le Sueur 2012: 37–58; Gill et al. 2016). From these various sources three design principles will be highlighted here as relevant to the drafting of the new legislation.

Avoid Juridification of the PSO Office Through Over-Prescription

As the previous sections have suggested, if PSO legislation is written too briefly it may not establish a sufficiently clear structure of authority. Question marks will subsequently arise as to how powers should be used and channelled, criticisms of the PSO's actions may be harder to defend and legal actions against the office may become necessary to clarify the law. By contrast, if the legislation is written in too much detail, then it may inappropriately confine the PSO, add unnecessary bureaucratic costs to decision-making and generate future pressure for amendment. In turn, these amendments will be delayed by the normal pressures of identifying legislative time for administrative justice reform.

There is also a long-standing concern in the sector that the desire for legislative control should not be pushed too far in the direction of formalising the decision-making processes away from the flexible and equitable model of dispute resolution it was designed for. What has been referred to as the 'pathology of legalism' in part describes a good-willed tendency to saturate the ombud model with procedural definition, aimed at ensuring that the ombud prioritises and safeguards the individual complainant, whilst preventing the office from over-reaching its powers.

The extent to which this is a live concern amongst the ombuds targeted for integration into the proposed new scheme is open for debate, but two geographically close examples illustrate the real risks contained in over-legislating. The Legal Profession and Legal Aid (Scotland) Act 2007 introduced the Scottish Legal Complaints Commission (SLCC), which was amended considerably at the Bill stage under the influence of the legal community. The end product is the longest of all complaint-handling legislation in the UK, providing specific detail at every stage of the SLCC's decision-making process (Scottish Legal Complaints Commission 2016: 5). A demonstrable outcome of this design is that the SLCC regularly complains about the 'highly detailed and legalistic drafting of the Act' (ibid.) which has added cost and time to decision-making. One issue has been the imposition of disproportionate decision-making practices locked in time. A similar story of 'over-lawyering' can be told about the Garda Síochána Ombudsman Commission—the PSO responsible for the police in Ireland (Garda Síochána Ombudsman Commission 2017: 4–5).

Allow Space for Grassroots Innovation

The experience of the SLCC also illustrates the danger of providing insufficient room for a scheme to adjust its practices according to experience. In its view:

> New legislation must take the form of a 'framework' Act and not prescribe administrative processes in the primary legislation. This is essential for future agility and ensuring proportionate regulation. (SLCC 2016: 5)

Thus whilst it might appear tempting to strive for certainty in legislation, an alternative approach is to provide the PSO with broad discretionary powers, but also accompany such powers with a corresponding duty to provide guidance on the manner in which that power is to be exercised. A benefit with this approach is that guidance can later be much more easily amended, as experience requires, subject to ongoing scrutiny and used as a benchmark against which exercises of the power can be tested. For instance, while the test of administrative fault might remain focused on the broad categories of 'maladministration' and 'service failure', the PSO might usefully be placed under a duty to provide further guidance on what those tests entail.[6]

Control Through Oversight and Transparency Rather Than Prescription

An objection to the 'framework' approach to legislation is that it leaves too much left unsaid. Here the broad concerns are that an overpowered PSO might suffer from mission creep and over-reach itself, and so compromise the delivery of its core function, complaint-handling. The answer here, however, is to build into the scheme's design strong and meaningful layers of oversight.

> Grievance-handlers should be held to account for their work. A design of a grievance handling system should facilitate accountability by considering the methods of accountability and the 'audience'. The appropriate mix of accountability mechanisms varies according to the context in which a grievance system operates. (Bondy and Le Sueur 2012: 37)

Thus, not only should the onus be placed on the PSO to provide further detail on the manner in which its powers are exercised through the publication of guidance, but also it should be obliged to evidence its delivery of its functions and duties. This issue is developed further in Chap. 9, but will include reporting duties, audit, parliamentary oversight, the deployment and internal monitoring of various service standards and performance indicators, as well as the internal tools discussed in the previous section.

Rather than signifying legal immaturity, this framework approach denotes a more honest reflection of our inability to agree what is the optimum role or method for the PSO. The fluidity of the position allows space for permanent disagreement and challenge as to the optimality of the choices made by the PSO. Whereas this may raise a concern about PSO performance, provided that scrutiny and transparency is strong, then it is unlikely that major or minor misuses of power will operate for long, which is the ordinary objection to broad discretionary powers. Further, performance is a matter that is better dealt with through flexible oversight than prescription.

[6] Most ombuds already provide such information.

Conclusion

This chapter has detailed a series of reform proposals, many of which are already included in the draft Bill but others are currently omitted. Much of the more forward-thinking practice in the sector has occurred as a result of ombud innovation, rather than being driven by legislation. This reputation-enhancing tendency in the sector evidences an acute concern for finding ways to defend a line on ombud standards, and illustrates the benefits of retaining a degree of operational discretion in the hands of the office-holder. The recommendation in this chapter is that as and when PSO legislation is updated, to signal the value of these new methods and to iron out minor clarifications of office's power, these new methods should be integrated into law.

In embedding such practices into PSO legislation, however, the duty should be placed on the office to provide guidance on how they will be deployed and reporting duties should be an embedded feature of the reformed ombud model. Overall, the new PSO legislation should aim to be bold, but offset by arrangements for transparency and strong oversight.

References

The Bach Commission. (2017). *The Right to Justice*. London: Fabian Society.

Bondy, V., & Le Sueur, A. (2012). *Designing Redress: A Study About Grievances Against Public Bodies*. London: Public Law Project.

Cabinet Office. (2016). *Draft Public Service Ombudsman Bill*. Cm. 9374.

Civil Justice Council. (2018). *ADR and Civil Justice*. Retrieved November 7, 2019, from https://www.judiciary.uk/wp-content/uploads/2018/12/CJC-ADRWG-Report-FINAL-Dec-2018.pdf.

Communities and Local Government Committee. (2012–2013). *The Work of the Local Government Ombudsman* HC 431.

Creutzfeldt, N. (2016). A Voice for Change? The Trust Relationships Between Ombudsmen, Individuals and Public Service Providers. *Journal of Social Welfare and Family Law, 38*(4), 460–479.

Dispute Resolution Ombudsman. (2018). *Rules of Full Membership*. Retrieved November 7, 2019, from https://www.thefurnitureombudsman.org/_documents/rules-of-membership.pdf.

Financial Ombudsman Service. (2011). *Transparency and the Financial Ombudsman Service: Publishing Ombudsman Decisions, Next Steps*. Retrieved November 7, 2019, from https://www.financial-ombudsman.org.uk/files/17772/publishing-decisions-sep11.pdf.

Fiss, O. M. (1984). Against Settlement. *Yale Law Journal, 93*, 1073.

Garda Síochána Ombudsman Commission. (2017). *Proposal for Legislative Change: Submission to the Department for Justice and Equality*. Retrieved November 7, 2019, from https://www.gardaombudsman.ie/publications/other-reports/.

Genn, H. (2012). What Is Civil Justice For? Reform, ADR, and Access to Justice. *Yale Journal of Law and the Humanities, 24*(1), 397.

Gill, C., & Creutzfeldt, N. (2018). The 'Ombuds Watchers': Collective Dissent and Legal Protest Amongst Users of Public Services Ombuds. *Social and Legal Studies, 27*(3), 367–388.

Gill, C., Williams, J., Brennan, C., & Hirst, C. (2016). Designing Consumer Redress: A Dispute System Design (DSD) Model for Consumer-to-Business Disputes. *Legal Studies, 36*(3), 438–463.

Harlow, C. (2018). Ombudsmen: 'Hunting Lions' or 'Swatting Flies'. In M. Hertogh & R. Kirkham (Eds.), *Research Handbook on the Ombudsman*. Cheltenham: Edward Elgar.

Housing Ombudsman. (2018a). *Guidance on Reviews of Determinations*. Retrieved November 7, 2019, from https://www.housing-ombudsman.org.uk/wp-content/uploads/2018/09/Guidance-on-reviews-of-determinations.pdf.

Housing Ombudsman. (2018b). *Response to 'A New Deal for Social Housing Green Paper'*. Retrieved November 7, 2019, from https://www.housing-ombudsman.org.uk/wp-content/uploads/2018/11/Housing-Ombudsman-Service-response-to-Green-Paper-website-version.pdf.

Kirkham, R., & Stuhmcke, A. (forthcoming). The Common Law Theory and Practice of the Ombudsman/Judiciary Relationship. *Common Law World Review*.

Koo, A. (2018). The Role of the English Courts in Alternative Dispute Resolution. *Legal Studies, 38*, 666–683.

Law Commission. (2010–2011). *Public Services Ombudsmen*. HC 1136.

Local Government and Social Care Ombudsman. (2019). *Decisions Website* Retrieved November 7, 2019, from https://www.lgo.org.uk/decisions.

Neuberger, L. (2010). *Equity, ADR, Arbitration and the Law: Different Dimensions of JUSTICE* (Keating Lecture, Lincoln's Inn). Retrieved November 7, 2019, from https://www.innertemplelibrary.com/2010/05/equity-adr-arbitration-and-the-law-different-dimensions-of-justice-speech-by-lord-neuberger-of-abbotsbury/.

PHSO. (2009). *Principles of Good Administration*. Retrieved November 7, 2019, from https://www.ombudsman.org.uk/about-us/our-principles/principles-good-administration.

PHSO. (2018). *PHSO Business Plan 2018–19*.Retrieved November 7, 2019, from https://www.ombudsman.org.uk/publications/our-business-plan-2018-19.

SPSO. (2018). *Customer Service Complaints Procedure.* Retrieved November 7, 2019, from https://archive.spso.org.uk/sites/spsoarchive/files/communications_material/leaflets_public/general/SPSO%20Customer%20Service%20Complaints%20Procedure.pdf.

Scottish Legal Complaints Commission. (2016). *#Reimagine Regulation: Priorities for a Consultation on Legal Services Regulation.* Retrieved November 7, 2019, from https://www.scottishlegalcomplaints.org.uk/3016.

CHAPTER 9

The Challenges of Independence, Accountability and Governance in the Ombudsman Sector

Brian Thompson

Abstract This chapter explores the continuing challenge of holding to account an institution, the proposed Public Service Ombudsman (PSO), which is itself a mechanism of accountability, while ensuring its independence is not impaired. The model of Officers of Parliament, as developed in the UK and New Zealand, is used as the template for an examination of the provisions in the draft Public Service Ombudsman Bill. While these provisions draw heavily on the first official to be considered an Officer of Parliament, the Comptroller and Auditor General, there are variations relating to the arrangements for appointment and corporate governance. As well as suggesting specific changes to the draft legislative provisions, the conclusions recommend a wider debate on both (a) Officers of Parliament as a distinct unit of our constitutional watchdogs and (b) best practice in corporate governance in the ombudsman sector.

B. Thompson (✉)
University of Liverpool, Liverpool, UK
e-mail: wbt@liverpool.ac.uk

R. Kirkham, C. Gill (eds.), *A Manifesto for Ombudsman Reform*,
https://doi.org/10.1007/978-3-030-40612-7_9

Keywords Ombudsman • Independence • Accountability • Parliamentary oversight • Corporate governance

Introduction

It is almost universally agreed that the ombud institution must be independent of government in the job of handling and determining people's complaints about bodies delivering public services (e.g. *Venice Principles on the Ombudsman* (Council of Europe 2019)). It is also agreed that the institution must be accountable for its performance of this work and that, for public services ombuds (PSO), Parliament should play a role in ensuring the ombud's independence and accountability as part of its work of holding the government and public bodies to account. This seems promising, especially when in the draft 2016 Public Service Ombudsman Bill, Scheds. 1–3, (the 'draft Bill'), for the new PSO it appears that there is also some agreement about adopting or adapting the scrutiny arrangements from another officer charged with holding public administration to account on behalf of Parliament, the Comptroller and Auditor General (C&AG) and the National Audit Office (NAO) (PASC 2014; Gordon 2014).

The position on accountability is complicated, however, as the proposals in the draft Bill are novel and the topic of corporate governance is under-scrutinised in ombudsman literature. Indeed, they were considered in only one of the background reports which led to the draft Bill (Gordon 2014). New proposals on corporate governance though play an important part in the draft legislation's provisions on accountability which have the aim of providing assurance and engendering public confidence in the PSO's performance. A lack of such public confidence was strikingly demonstrated in the announcement by a group, the Patients Association, when based on the experience of its members it said that it could not recommend resort to the Parliamentary and Health Ombudsman (PHSO) for those complaining about the NHS in England (Patients Association 2014).[1]

This chapter assumes that the delivery of accountability plays out on a number of different levels with the PSO. Chapters 7 and 8 considered the issue of procedural fairness as a way of securing confidence in complaint handling. In this sense, accountability of ombud decision-making can only

[1] Subsequently in 2018 the Patients Association announced that it had welcomed changes which the PHSO had made but that more progress was still required and that it would work with the PHSO to secure it (Patients Association 2018).

be partial because it is meant to be the second and final stage in the complaints handling process. Rightly, Parliamentary committees will not consider cases where the user of the PSO service has been dissatisfied with the outcome due to concerns about encroaching upon the office's independence. Further, for such cases the merits of the decision are usually excluded from legal challenge. This means that only limited reconsideration of PSO decision-making is possible and judicial review is confined to legal errors, and costs preclude this option for most dissatisfied users.

Internal reconsideration is also part of accountability and Kirkham's proposal in Chap. 8 to build on non-statutory developments and amend the legislation to require the PSO to review both service and decisions is sensible; however, there will have to be some criteria to manage the numbers, especially of reviews of decisions, and this practice will need to be reported on. Transparency and engagement with users and other stakeholders are, I would argue, also part of the overall arrangements for accountability and I support the proposal for a Quality Assurance Board to be incorporated into the ombudsman design to aid such oversight.

The aforementioned layers of scrutiny are important, but oversight of performance, particularly Parliamentary oversight, remains an important part of the solution to securing public confidence. Towards this end, in the following section I argue that the Officers of Parliament model is the main device that has been applied to the new PSO in order to secure accountability. This model is used in the chapter to analyse the draft Bill's provisions on independence, accountability and governance. A key concern identified here is that the draft Bill is an attempt to develop ad hoc reform to a pre-existing model, which is leading to inconsistency in the way in which Parliament manages different Parliamentary Officers. These inconsistencies risk causing problems in the oversight of the new PSO. Another key concern that deserves further inquiry is the novelty of the corporate governance solution to the ombud sector.

The Officers of Parliament Model

The Officers of Parliament model is one in which accountability institutions are set up as statutory officers, who require independence from the executive and have a special relationship with Parliament (Buck et al. 2011: ch. 6). The Officers of Parliament model secures independence from the executive by vesting in Parliament the powers to appoint, remove and resource the Officer. Additionally, the model builds-in a natural division of labour to provide the necessary external oversight of the relevant

Officer. This potential requires Parliament to be sufficiently involved in the work of the Officer to undertake proper scrutiny and also be sufficiently distant to respect its independence in directing the work of the institution.

The nature of the Parliamentary relationship is multi-faceted. The functions which Parliamentary committees could conduct in their relationships with Parliamentary Officers include *sponsorship* (appointment, removal, budget setting); *scrutiny* (holding to account); and *support*. With the PSO, the latter function would capture primarily Parliamentary support for the office when a recommendation to remedy the injustice caused by maladministration is not being complied with by the executive, but may also cover other instances of the executive leaning on the ombudsman. Such support is a two-way street, however, as the work of the PSO can also assist Parliamentarians in holding the executive to account by complementing their work in both resolving grievances and scrutinising the executive.

A good example of the Officers of Parliament model being applied is New Zealand, which has designated three Officers of Parliament,[2] whose functions contribute to the core purposes of a Parliament. The New Zealand model splits the three main aspects of the Parliament/Officer of Parliament relationship between entirely separate supporting committees. Thus under legislation there is a framework of (a) general sponsorship of three Officers of Parliament by an all-party Officers of Parliament Committee chaired by the Speaker; (b) scrutiny of those three officers by three separate subject-specific committees, as part of the Parliamentary annual review of governmental and public bodies; and (c) the provision of support for that regular financial review by committees using Audit Office briefings and also in committees' inquiries where they may be following-up the reports of Controller and Auditor General's audits and Ombudsman New Zealand's investigations (Buchanan 2008; Ferguson 2010).

In the UK, however, the development of the Officer in Parliament model has been more narrowly focused around just two institutions, the C&AG and the Parliamentary Ombudsman, and no one organised model exists. At Westminster, the model originated with the Exchequer and Audit Departments Act 1866 which consolidated departments and created the C&AG. This arrangement became more sophisticated when the

[2] The Ombudsman, the Parliamentary Commissioner for the Environment and the Controller and Auditor General, see Ferguson (2010).

National Audit Act 1983 created the National Audit Office (NAO) led by the C&AG, and formally confirmed the C&AG as an Officer of Parliament (s.1(2) and PAC 2008). The 1983 Act also established a new House of Commons committee, the Public Accounts Commission (the Commission), which had the functions of approving the annual estimates of the NAO, as well as appointing its accounting officer and auditor. The Budget Responsibility and National Audit Act 2011 (the BRNA Act 2011) later made the NAO a corporate body and provided for a corporate governance regime by way of a statutory Board which is overseen by the Commission.

The 2011 legislation is the model for the draft Bill which will now be analysed. However, as will be explained below, in some respects it provides a more confused solution than the more structured New Zealand model, which in turn raises a number of concerns.

Parliamentary Sponsorship: Appointment, Removal, Tenure and Remuneration

The independence of a PSO is promoted by appropriate arrangements for appointment, removal, tenure and remuneration. All these functions are facilitated by the Officers in Parliament model and are appropriately supported by the draft Bill. The draft Bill mainly replicates existing arrangements in the UK and largely conforms to international best practices, as most recently detailed in the *Venice Principles on the Ombudsman* (Council of Europe 2019: Articles 3, 10). Tenure is a single term of seven years and the salary is linked to that of judicial office-holders which is paid out of the Consolidated Fund (Sched. 1, paras. 1 and 3). The provision for removal on an address to the Queen from both Houses of Parliament is unchanged (Sched. 1, para. 2) but differs slightly from the provisions in the legislation in Scotland, Wales and Northern Ireland. In those jurisdictions the motion to remove the PSO requires the support of at least two-thirds of the seats in the Parliament or Assemblies, whereas at Westminster a simple majority is sufficient.[3] On this point, the *Venice Principles* state that 'The parliamentary majority required for removal … shall be equal to, and preferably higher than, the one required for election' (Council of Europe 2019: Article 11). None of the UK jurisdictions stipulate a specified majority

[3] Scottish Public Services Ombudsman Act 2010, Sched. 1, para. 4; Public Services Ombudsman Act (Northern Ireland) 2016, Sched. 1, para. 9; Public Services Ombudsman (Wales) Act 2019, Sched. 1, para. 3(4)–(5).

vote for appointment but otherwise they meet the *Venice Principles* on appointment including a public, open, merit-based procedure provided by law in Article 11.

While the draft Bill slightly increases the Parliamentary role on appointment, there are some modifications when compared to the model under the 1967 Act and that developed for the C&AG. This is not an uncommon aspect in incremental reform but is one which has deliberately avoided a uniform approach to designing Officers in Parliament. For instance, the Commission would now have an important role overseeing both the C&AG and the PSO. Whereas the Commission is not involved in appointing the C&AG, however, its approval is required for the moving of the motion to appoint the PSO, as is a recommendation for appointment by the chair of the proposed PSO Board (Sched. 1, para. 1 and Sched. 2, para. 2, respectively). By contrast, for the C&AG the motion to appoint as moved by the PM must have the consent of the chair of another select committee, the Public Accounts Committee (PAC), who is also an ex officio member of the Commission (BRNA Act 2011, s. 11). A justification for this difference would appear to be that the Chair of PAC has a symbolically important role, providing Parliamentary balance as by convention he/she is a member of the main opposition party. The chair of PAC also has a close working relationship with the C&AG, both when his/her committee follows up reports produced by the NAO and when the committee takes evidence in its inquiries on those reports, with the C&AG attending as a standing witness at these sessions.

To emphasise the Parliamentary connection, another adopted process from existing practice towards multiple statutory officers could be confirmed in legislation. Both the current PHSO and the C&AG attend a pre-hearing appointment hearings designed to involve Parliament in significant public appointments made by ministers. If the select committee's examination of the preferred candidate's professional competence and personal independence does not lead to their endorsement, this does not bind the minister (Secretary of State for Justice 2007: 27–28) but can be highly influential. Currently the appointment of the PHSO involves a pre-appointment hearing held by Public Administration and Constitutional Affairs Committee (PACAC) and at the last appointment, this was held jointly with the (then) Health Committee which supplied three of the total of seven members who conducted the hearing (Health & PACAC 2017). In Scotland and Northern Ireland there is no such hearing, perhaps because they are Parliamentary managed processes, but Wales which also has a Parliamentary managed appointment procedure incorporated a pre-appointment hearing for the first time in 2014.

Parliamentary Scrutiny and Support

In the Westminster system the functions of scrutinising and supporting the work of the Officer in Parliament tend to overlap. Scrutiny is partially addressed by the draft Bill, whereas support is not directly dealt with.

Scrutiny is most obviously provided for when budgets are agreed. Currently the PHSO negotiates its budget direct with the Treasury and the Local Government and Social Care Ombudsman (LGSCO) with the Ministry for Housing, Communities and Local Government. By contrast, the draft Bill provides for the Commission to approve (a) the PSO Board's estimates, which is the annual budgetary process in which the spending plans are presented, and (b) the forward planning which comprises the initial functions and resources strategy and then its revisions (Sched. 2, para. 22). The Commission may approve these plans with or without modifications and in both of these scrutiny exercises the Treasury provides material for the Commission to consider. The Commission may also direct a Value for Money (VFM) examination of the PSO to be conducted by the C&AG (Sched. 2, para. 19(6)). Similarly, the Commission may direct a VFM of the C&AG to be conducted by an independent external auditor (BRNA Act 2011 Sched. 2, para. 6). Such examinations are not about the merits or accuracy of the audit or complaint determinations made by the C&AG or the PSO and their staff. Instead they consider the economy, efficiency and effectiveness of how they conduct their work. On this point, the draft Bill has adopted the provisions in the 2011 statute for the Commission's scrutiny of the NAO.

One issue that is left blank by the draft Bill is the role of the annual review of the new PSO. At present, the PHSO has an annual session with the PACAC, following up the publication of the PHSO's annual report and accounts. This committee has previously expressed a desire to move away from scrutinising the PHSO to using its reports to hold the Government's public administration to account (PASC 2014). If PACAC's practice of examining the work of the PHSO in an annual evidence session were not to apply to the new PSO, this might mean a significant reduction in Parliamentary scrutiny. This may be the outcome if scrutiny is left to the Commission, because the practice of this particular committee in its scrutiny of the NAO's estimates on spending and forward planning, and the functions and resources strategy, is that it tends not to look back on past performance. Again there is a difference here with the C&AG, as in addition to the Commission's approval of the estimates, another committee, PAC, also considers the estimates and passes on its views to the Commission. Unless the Commission changes its practices, for deeper scrutiny PACAC may need to continue this annual review function. This latter practice is the one followed in New Zealand, where specialised subject committees conduct annual performance reviews of relevant government departments and particular public bodies, including the three Officers of Parliament (New Zealand Parliament 2018). In the annual review the committees seek a briefing from the Controller & Auditor General which helps them decide the degree of detail or a particular aspect which they will focus upon. The committees can use relevant reports of Ombudsman New Zealand to assist them in conducting annual reviews and particular inquiries.

In terms of supporting the work of the PHSO, PACAC has since 2014 increased the numbers of inquiries following-up PHSO reports, aiming to act as the PAC does with the C&AG. It could expand this work itself (although the remit of this committee is very wide going well beyond the PHSO remit) and redirect some reports to relevant sister select committees for their follow-up action. But if this follow-up work were to lead to PACAC stopping its annual review of the work of the PHSO, then there is a danger that the degree of Parliamentary scrutiny would be lessened. This reduction in focus is unlikely to be compensated for even if the Commission conducted its two annual sessions in approving the estimates and the strategy, and could order VFM examinations. The New Zealand model of the sponsorship and scrutiny roles being conducted by two committees—sponsorship, estimates and strategy by the Officers of Parliament Committee and annual review by a select committee—provides more scrutiny than the present arrangements for the C&AG and those proposed for the PSO.

One final point to highlight is that the Commission has the Leader of the House of Commons as an ex officio member. It does seem odd that a minister is a member of the body approving estimates and strategy of the C&AG and, in the future, the PSO. Possibly a recognition of this incongruity explains the practice of the last three years in which the minister has sent apologies for meetings and not participated in their scrutiny of the C&AG. It is surely preferable that no minister is a member of the Commission.

Corporate Governance

Corporate governance thinking has entered into the ombudsman landscape in recent times. It seeks to provide for more effective governance of private and public bodies by establishing a board to oversee the organisation, composed of executive members supported and challenged by non-executive members who bring experience and expertise. In particular the Board contributes to forward planning, and overseeing audit and risk, remuneration and appointments. Currently most PSOs are corporations sole with power invested in a single office-holder who, in recent years, have tended to appoint non-statutory non-executives to provide advice. The draft Bill would for the first time embed this structure in legislation. In this section I first detail the proposed arrangements, before offering a critique.

Board Composition

The draft Bill gives the Board the principal duty of providing the PSO with staff and resources to carry out its statutory functions (cl. 3(2)). There are to be more non-executive members than executive members (Sched. 2, para. 1(3)). One of the non-executives is the chair who is appointed by the Queen on a motion moved by the PM and agreed to by the Commission (Sched. 2, para. 2). The chair would recommend other non-executive members for appointment by the Commission which can specify terms (Sched. 2, para. 4). The non-executive members would be appointed for up to three years and could be reappointed for a second term of up to three years by the Commission but an extension for the chair is made by the Queen on the PM's recommendation (Sched. 2, paras. 2–5). The chief executive of the Board is the PSO but the non-executive members may appoint an employee of the Board, which must be approved by the Commission (Sched. 2, para. 10). The chief executive is the accounting officer for the Board (Sched. 2, para. 10(3)). The chief executive recommends other executive members for appointment by the non-executive members who may accept or reject in which case another recommendation is made (Sched. 2, para. 11).

The chair of the Board may be dismissed, like the PSO, by the Queen following an address by both Houses of Parliament (respectively Sched. 2, para. 9(1); Sched. 1, para. 2(3)) but the grounds are not stated which fails to meet the *Venice Principles* (Council of Europe 2019: Article 11). This anomaly needs to be addressed.

Board Functions

The Board provides staffing and services for the conduct of the PSO's functions (cl.3(2)). Schedule 2, paras. 19–22, deal with accounts, audit, annual report, estimates and strategy. The chief executive prepares on behalf of the Board the annual resource accounts which are audited by the C&AG whose report is sent to the Commission which lays the accounts and the C&AG's report before Parliament. The chief executive prepares an annual report on the conduct of the Board's functions which must include details about the time taken to investigate complaints, how many investigations were not completed within 12 months and the action taken to ensure that the 12-months target is met.

The Board must prepare its annual estimates and forward plans for approval by the Commission. The initial functions and resources strategy is submitted before the first estimates and the strategy must be reviewed at least every 12 months and each revision must be approved by the Commission. The estimates and strategy may be approved with or without modifications by the Commission. Copies of these documents must be sent to the Treasury so it may offer comments for the Commission's consideration. Indeed the Commission is required to consult the Treasury on the estimates and take into account any representations.

The Board under Schedule 2, paras. 23 and 24, has monitoring and review duties. It monitors the carrying out of the PSO's statutory functions, with particular reference to the quality and efficiency of the service provided by the PSO and the desirability of improving that service. This monitoring is to be conducted in accordance with a scheme prepared by the Board and approved by the Commission, and revised in accordance with representations made by the Commission. The Board must inform the Commission of any findings it makes in the exercise of this monitoring duty but the Commission cannot question the merits of action taken by the PSO in a particular case.

The Board must conduct triennial reviews on the operation of the Act. The reports of these reviews, with any recommendations or conclusions, are to be submitted to the Commission which is to lay them before Parliament. The Board must also submit the reports to a minister or any designated authority that is a body within the jurisdiction of the PSO.

Protecting PSO Independence

The PSO must make a declaration in the annual report as to whether he/she has been able to carry out the office's functions independently (Sched. 2, para. 21(4)). Schedule 3 provides for relations between the PSO and the Board. The Board is to produce a code of practice on relations between the PSO and the Board. The PSO and Commission will be consulted in the preparation and reviews of the code. The Commission approves the code and its revisions and lays them before Parliament. The code with which the Board and PSO must comply must (a) set out how the Board will secure the need for the PSO to carry out functions independently when discharging its duty of providing staff and resources for the PSO; (b) include provision for the preparation, review and revision of the annual report, the Board's estimates and strategy, the monitoring scheme for the PSO and reports following the triennial reviews of the operation of the statute; and (c) may make provision on the management of the Board's affairs with regard to guidance on management of public bodies and on such other matters as the Board thinks appropriate.

Assessment of the Corporate Governance Proposals

Before considering the corporate governance details of the draft Bill, there is the issue as to whether or not the PSO should be the chief executive. The draft presumes it but another employee can be appointed with the Commission's approval (Sched. 2, para. 10). Gordon argued that the current position under the corporation sole structure, where the ombud is chief ombud, chief executive and chair of the Board, is confusing and one person should not be filling each of those roles (Gordon 2014). He concluded that in a body the size of the PSO, separation of roles is required along the usual corporate lines of non-executive chair and chief executive.

However, I would argue that the public and Parliament expect the ombud to be responsible as the ombud personifies the organisation. The PSO should be the accounting officer with its direct reporting relationship to Parliament. Is it necessary for that role to be attached to the title chief executive? A solution might be available from the 2011 legislation for the C&AG, which provides that the C&AG is to be the NAO's chief executive (Sched. 2, para. 11) but also authorises the Commission to appoint the chief executive or some other appropriate person as the accounting officer for the NAO (Sched. 2, para. 24). Perhaps consideration of the roles of chief executive and accounting officer on the PSO Board could lead to a redistribution between a chief executive, who might be more of a chief operating officer, and the PSO as accounting officer with the direct responsibility to Parliament.

Adopting this approach could take account of the unusual nature of the work of complaints resolution. For example, when considering the quality and efficiency of casework how easy is it to attribute responsibility? If an investigator fails to follow protocol, or takes too long, is that individual fault or a failure of internal quality assurance? What if there has been an unexpected surge in complaints and new staff have been hired but the budget cannot accommodate both the increase in staffing and the extra training required? Is the PSO as independent officer responsible for training and the quality assurance or is that a responsibility of the Board? Can arguments about supposed 'under-funding' excuse blame? What if the non-executives determined that it would not be prudent to seek supplementary estimates, or if they were requested in estimates submitted by the Board and not approved by the Commission?

It is suggested that the issue of the PSO's responsibility is similar to debates in relation to ministerial accountability and responsibility. More recent thinking is that although a minister is required to account for all the actions of departmental officials, they are not necessarily responsible. This contrasts with an older view that the minister would be responsible unless the actions were completely outside the scope of the official's normal work. The difficulty is that there are grey areas, which can be reduced but not eliminated by careful detailing of the ministers' and officials' responsibilities in the Framework Documents establishing Government agencies (Public Service Committee 1996).

Similarly, the production of a code of practice to govern the relationship between the PSO and the Board, and the Board's scheme for monitoring the conduct of PSO functions, will be extremely important. The example of the code of practice on the relationship between the C&AG and the NAO Board demonstrates the difficulty. There is some detail fleshing out the statutory provisions, but despite the Commission's hopes that corporate governance arrangements must deal with disagreements, a provision in the code covers the situation where the C&AG is seeking additional funds for work which has to be approved by the Board. It sets out options and simply states 'The NAO Board will consider the C&AG's proposals and agree a way forward' (NAO 2012).

The C&AG's relationship with the NAO Board is different from that between the PSO and the Board because the legislation gives the C&AG complete discretion in statutory auditing and VFM examinations of departments and other public bodies. This is reflected in the joint responsibility of the C&AG and the NAO Board in producing the estimates and the strategy. By contrast, with the PSO the final responsibility for the estimates and strategy rests with the PSO Board and its non-executive majority.

There needs to be a wider debate about the details of the corporate governance arrangements and the relationship between the PSO and the Board. Are there good reasons why the C&AG has joint responsibility for estimates and strategy and the PSO does not? Is the declaration by the PSO on whether or not he/she was able to carry out the statutory functions independently a useful safeguard or so drastic that it would not be used? Does the Parliamentary appointment of the chair of the Board confer legitimacy and power sufficient to deter a PSO from 'going rogue', or does it set up rival sources of power blurring rather than clarifying lines of responsibility?

Finally there is the issue of review in two respects: (a) regular reviews of the operation of the statute and (b) ad hoc independent peer reviews. The Board has a duty to conduct a triennial review of the operation of the Act (Sched. 2, para. 23). This could be more useful than the similar provision in the LGSCO legislation (Local Government Act 1974, s.23(12)) as the report goes to the Commission and increases the possibility of action being taken if the Commission supported its recommendations. This provision could be made more meaningful if there was a duty to stage a strategic review of the institution on a septennial basis, given that the tenure of the PSO is now a single seven year term (Buck et al. 2011: 186). The bigger strategic review can take a more fundamental examination than the internal triennial operation reviews, and with at least two Parliamentary select committees engaged with the institution, progress in reform might possibly happen more timeously.

By way of precedent, two select committees have recommended independent peer reviews focusing on the quality of decision-making and review in the LGSCO (Communities & Local Government Committee 2012) and the robustness of financial planning and control in the PHSO (PACAC 2018). Both reviews were commissioned and were constructively critical (Thomas et al. 2013; Tyndall et al. 2018) and were considered positively by the relevant select committees. PACAC in following up the latter review recommended that (a) it be repeated every three to four years, (b) relevant professional expertise outside the ombud sector should also be used to bolster the value of such a review's conclusions; and (c) to engage with PHSO service users and stakeholders to supplement and complement other forms of customer satisfaction data (PACAC 2019). The committee appeared to be suggesting that the idea of using both peer reviewers and other professionals is good as together the arrangement provides expertise and credibility. It is of course important that users and stakeholders are involved. Teams of reviewers from peer and other backgrounds could conduct not only triennial operation and septennial strategic reviews but also ad hoc reviews on a particular issue which would benefit from such consideration.

Conclusions

When the draft Bill is considered by Parliament, there will be an opportunity to have a wider debate about two items arising from its provisions for independence and accountability: the role and organisation of those constitutional watchdogs known as Officers of Parliament; and their corporate governance arrangements.

Some years ago the Public Administration Select Committee (PASC) conducted an inquiry into the organisation and accountability of the ethical regulators' landscape (PASC 2007). The recommendations came to naught perhaps because the project was too large, including regulators appointed by the executive as well as watchdogs. This chapter has argued that the Officers of Parliament model should be adhered to more consistently, and like the C&AG, and following New Zealand, the PSO should be statutorily designated an Officer of Parliament and that certain implications follow from that designation. It is suggested that the Commission should be renamed as the Public Accounts and Public Administration Commission to reflect its broadened role, and consideration given to whether its chair should be from the official opposition. The current ex officio members of the Commission, the minister and the chair of the PAC, should be removed. The latter, like the chair of PACAC, should be involved in the selection of the C&AG and the PSO respectively and the Commission should conduct the pre-appointment hearings for those officers. Consideration should be given to the degree of Parliamentary scrutiny of the work of the PSO and whether the New Zealand model of separation of sponsorship and scrutiny should be followed with the

Commission approving the estimates and the strategy but PACAC conducting a deeper scrutiny of the past year's work.

Corporate governance did not really feature in the consultation on policy before the draft legislation. Given that there are different perspectives with different logics, managerial, constitutional and legal, there should be an examination of the differences in the proposed arrangements for the PSO and its Board and those of the C&AG and the NAO Board. Consideration should be given to whether those differences are justified and how a wider range of powers and responsibilities, such as a complaints standard role, would be accommodated in such governance arrangements.

VFM examinations of the PSO are a good idea but consideration should be given to ensuring the PSO Board can commission peer reviews of its operations. Ombud peer reviewers could be members of mixed professional and peer reviewers conducting VFM examinations and the triennial operation and septennial strategic reviews which should report to the Commission and the Board.

Finally it is surely time for Parliament to consider allowing select committees to initiate legislation. Committees in the Assemblies in Northern Ireland and Wales conducted inquiries on ombud reform and consulted on draft legislation, which they then shepherded through the legislative process to enactment in 2016 and 2019 respectively. Such a move would allow Parliament to maximise its support of its Parliamentary Officers.

References

Buchanan, R. (2008). Commonwealth Experience II – Officers of Parliament in Australia and New Zealand: Building a Working Model. In O. Gay & B. Winetrobe (Eds.), *Parliament's Watchdogs. At the Crossroads*. London: The Constitution Unit.

Buck, T., Kirkham, R., & Thompson, B. (2011). *The Ombudsman Enterprise and Administrative Justice*. Farnham: Ashgate Publishing.

Communities & Local Government Committee. (2012). *The Work of the Local Government Ombudsman* (HC 431 of 2012–13).

Council of Europe. (2019). European Commission for Democracy Through Law (Venice Commission), *Principles on the Protection and Promotion of the Ombudsman Institution* (CDL-AD(2019)005).

Ferguson, L. (2010). Parliament's Watchdogs—New Zealand's Officers of Parliament. *Australasian Parliamentary Review, 25*(2), 133–145.

Gordon, R. (2014). *Better to Serve the Public: Proposals to Restructure, Reform, Renew and Reinvigorate Public Services Ombudsmen*. London: Cabinet Office.

Health-Public Administration and Constitutional Affairs Committees. (2017). *Appointment of the Parliamentary and Health Service Ombudsman*. HC 810 (2016–17).
NAO. (2012). *National Audit Office, Code of Practice Dealing With the Relationship Between the National Audit Office and the Comptroller and Auditor General*. London: NAO.
New Zealand Parliament. (2018). *Annual Reviews Explained*. Retrieved October 17, 2019, from https://www.parliament.nz/en/visit-and-learn/how-parliament-works/fact-sheets/annual-reviews-explained/.
PAC. (2008). Committee of Public Accounts, *Holding Government to Account – 150 Years of the Committee of Public Accounts* (House of Commons).
PACAC. (2018). Public Administration and Constitutional Affairs Committee *PHSO Annual Scrutiny 2016–17* (HC 492 of 2017–19).
PACAC. (2019). Public Administration and Constitutional Affairs Committee, *PHSO Annual Scrutiny 2017/18: Towards a Modern and Effective Ombudsman Service* (HC 1855 of 2017–19).
PASC. (2007). Public Administration Select Committee *Ethics and Standards: The Regulation of Conduct in Public Life* (HC 121-1 of 2006–07).
PASC. (2014). Public Administration Select Committee *Time for a People's Ombudsman Service* (HC 655 of 2013–14).
Patients Association. (2014). *Parliamentary and Health Service Ombudsman: The People's Ombudsman How It Failed Us*. Retrieved September 6, 2019, from https://minhalexander.files.wordpress.com/2017/05/phso-the-peoples-ombudsman-how-it-failed-us-final4.pdf.
Patients Association. (2018). Position Statement: June 2018 PHSO. Retrieved September 6, 2019, from https://www.patients-association.org.uk/news/position-statement-phso.
Public Service Committee. (1996). *Ministerial Accountability and Responsibility*, (HC 313 of 1995–96).
Secretary of State for Justice and Lord Chancellor. (2007). *The Governance of Britain* (CM 7170).
Thomas, R, Martin, J., & Kirkham, R. (2013). *External Evaluation of the Local Government Ombudsman in England*. Retrieved September 6, 2019, from https://www.lgo.org.uk/assets/attach/2035/CLA-2008-Evaluation-of-the-LGO-The-Final-Report-2-2-.pdf.
Tyndall, P., Mitchell, C., & Gill, C. (2018). *Value for Money Study: Report of the Independent Peer Review of the Parliamentary and Health Service Ombudsman*. London: PHSO.

Index[1]

[1] Note: Page numbers followed by 'n' refer to notes.

R. Kirkham, C. Gill (eds.), *A Manifesto for Ombudsman Reform*,
https://doi.org/10.1007/978-3-030-40612-7

The manufacturer's authorised representative in the EU is Springer
Nature Customer Service Centre GmbH, Europaplatz 3, 69115 Heidelberg,
Germany. If you have any concerns regarding our products, please
contact ProductSafety@springernature.com

Printed and bound by CPI Group (UK) Ltd, Croydon, CR0 4YY
25/09/2026
02222902-0016